BROKEN
+BLESSED

An Invitation
to My Generation

FR. JOSHUA JOHNSON

FOREWORD BY
FR. MIKE SCHMITZ

ASCENSION

West Chester, Pennsylvania

Copyright © 2018 Ascension Publishing, LLC. All rights reserved.

With the exception of short excerpts used in articles and critical reviews, no part of this work may be reproduced, transmitted, or stored in any form whatsoever, printed or electronic, without the prior written permission of the publisher.

Excerpts from the English translation of the *Catechism of the Catholic Church* for use in the United States of America. Copyright © 1994, 1997, United States Catholic Conference, Inc.–Libreria Editrice Vaticana. All rights reserved.

Unless otherwise noted, Scripture passages are from the Revised Standard Version–Catholic Edition. Copyright © 1946, 1952, 1971, Division of Christian Education of the National Council of the Churches of Christ in the United States of America. All rights reserved.

Ascension
Post Office Box 1990
West Chester, PA 19380
1-800-376-0520
ascensionpress.com

Cover photo by Matt Pirrall

Printed in the United States of America

19 20 21 22 23 8 7 6 5 4

ISBN 978-1-945179-50-1

CONTENTS

FOREWORD v

CHAPTER ONE
Introduction: A Hospital for Sinners 1

CHAPTER TWO
Come, Follow Me 17

CHAPTER THREE
Who Told You That? 39

CHAPTER FOUR
Intimacy with God?. 67

CHAPTER FIVE
Breaking the Chains of Sin. 91

CHAPTER SIX
Reforming Community from Within 117

CHAPTER SEVEN
Prioritizing Prayer 137

EPILOGUE 161

APPENDIX: Praying the Rosary 163

FOREWORD

Several years ago, Fr. Josh Johnson and I were featured in the Ascension video *I Will Follow*, where we recounted our respective journeys to the priesthood. Perhaps not surprisingly, our stories are remarkably similar. We had both experienced the love of Jesus—a love which transformed our lives and led us to consider serving him as priests. We had both encountered obstacles in discerning our vocations. And, since ordination, we have both been living joyful lives as priests.

Since the release of *I Will Follow*, many people have asked me how I knew Fr. Josh and how long we have been friends. The truth is, prior to shooting the video, he and I had not even met! Since then, though, he and I have become good friends. As I have come to know and admire Fr. Josh, there is one word that immediately comes to mind to describe him: authenticity.

Let's reflect on that word for a moment. We say that a dollar bill is "authentic" when it is the genuine article, when it truly is what it represents. A counterfeit dollar is inauthentic; it is a misrepresentation … a lie, if you will. A counterfeit bill is inauthentic; it is not even worth the paper upon which it is printed. But an authentic bill is the "real thing," the "genuine article." It actually is what it claims to be.

There is an old Latin expression *esse quam videri* — "to be rather than to seem [or appear to be]," which is the motto of many educational institutions, several cities, and the state of North

Carolina. This is another way of saying, "Be authentic" ... "Be who you appear to be."

That describes Fr. Josh. And it accurately describes this book.

In *Broken and Blessed,* you will get an authentic, "inside look" into the heart and mind of a man who has fully given himself to Jesus Christ as his disciple and priest. In the years that I have known Fr. Josh, I have found him to be a true man of God, a true follower of Jesus. He is like the disciple Nathanael in the Gospel of John, of whom Jesus said: "Behold, an Israelite indeed, in whom is no guile!" (Guile is another word for duplicity, being of "two minds," of seeming to be one thing but really being another.) Fr. Josh is what he appears to be: a priest striving for an authentic, deep relationship with our Lord. He is an inspiring example of authenticity for all of us.

In these pages, Fr. Josh offers a powerful witness, based on his own life story, that it is our very "brokenness" that allows God to "bless" us in a wonderful, life-changing way. In our weakness, God makes us strong in his service—if we let him! Here, you will see what following Jesus as an intentional disciple looks like. By sharing his own experiences, both before and after he was ordained, Fr. Josh weaves a narrative around what every Catholic should know about the Faith, presenting practical ways to live it out every day.

It is my sincere hope that this book will be a *blessing* to you in your *brokenness!* While you may not think of yourself as "broken," I'm sure you feel a little less than perfect, right? It is this imperfection that shows our need for God and his grace. Jesus seeks to make you "perfect"—to help you become what he has made you to be. You only need to let him!

— *Fr. Mike Schmitz*

Chapter One

INTRODUCTION: A Hospital for Sinners

In my relatively short time as a Catholic priest, I have had the privilege of being invited into deep conversations about God and the Church with people from various backgrounds. These conversations have taken place in some of the most random places, including the Louisiana State University (LSU) stadium before a football game, the checkout line at supermarkets, and—my favorite—in a men's restroom. One of my most memorable conversations about God and the Church actually took place at a restaurant bar.

One Monday afternoon, I drove to Covington, Louisiana, to meet with my spiritual director, a hermit who resides on the campus of a Benedictine monastery and seminary college. After spiritual direction, I called a good friend of mine, Michael Lane, who is a professor at the seminary. It was his birthday, so I invited him to have a drink with me.

We met at a local restaurant and grabbed two seats at the bar. Within a few minutes of ordering our drinks, an elderly man approached us. "Excuse me," he asked. "Are you a real Catholic priest?" Since I am only thirty, I get this question often. Many assume that I must be a fraternity pledge in costume. I responded, "Yes sir! I am a Catholic priest." The man's strident tone surprised me. "I just want you to know," he said, "that the Catholic Church is the most corrupt institution on the face of the earth … and priests are the most corrupt individuals in the world." After he made his comments, he stood over me, staring at me silently. It was clear from his body language that he was not joking. So I paused for a moment before I responded, praying for the Holy Spirit to inspire me with the words that this man needed to hear.

After what seemed like a long pause, I responded, "Sir, I just want you to know that I agree with you, one hundred percent. The Catholic Church is indeed the most corrupt institution on the face of the earth, and its priests are the most corrupt individuals. I want you to know that you are looking at the most corrupt, broken, and imperfect Catholic priest there is."

The man was visibly shocked by this reply, as was my friend sitting at the bar. I went on to tell him, "Sir, although Catholic priests, religious brothers and sisters, and laity are broken, imperfect, and corrupt, Jesus still chooses to dwell with us. In fact, two thousand years ago, he chose twelve very broken, imperfect, and corrupt men to be his apostles. Since Jesus is fully human and fully divine, he knew all the ways his apostles were going to show their brokenness. He knew all of their sins, both those they had committed before he called them and all those they were going to commit in the future. But guess what? He still chose them."

I then shared Jesus' prediction to the apostle Peter at the Last Supper that he would soon deny he even knew Jesus:

> "Simon, Simon, behold, Satan demanded to have you, that he
> might sift you like wheat, but I have prayed for you that your

faith may not fail; and when you have turned again, strengthen your brethren." And he said to him, "Lord, I am ready to go with you to prison and to death." He said, "I tell you, Peter, the cock will not crow this day, until you three times deny that you know me" (Luke 22:31-34).

Within a few hours, Peter had indeed denied him three times. The Gospel of Luke conveys how Jesus was seized and led away to the house of the high priest. As Jesus was being taken away, Peter and the other apostles ran away in fear. They abandoned Jesus in his moment of persecution. Eventually, Peter began to follow the crowd that had taken Jesus. As he sat around a campfire, a woman recognized him as one of Jesus' followers, but Peter denied that he even knew him. Then, someone else asserted that he was a disciple of Christ, and again he denied that he was. An hour later, a third person claimed that he had seen Peter accompanying Jesus, but he again denied it. Then, a rooster crowed. At that point, Jesus was being led past him and looked him in the eye. Peter remembered Jesus' prediction, and he went out and wept (see Luke 22:54-62).

CHOOSING THE WEAK TO SHAME THE STRONG

Our faith teaches that Jesus, while having a human nature, is a divine Person, the Second Person of the Blessed Trinity. So he knew that Peter was going to deny him, yet he still chose him to be an apostle—actually the "prince of apostles," the first pope. But Peter was not the only apostle whom Jesus predicted would sin against him. Following the Last Supper, as they went out to the Mount of Olives, Jesus addressed the other apostles: "You will all fall away; for it is written, 'I will strike the shepherd, and the sheep will be scattered.' But after I am raised up, I will go before you to Galilee'" (Mark 14:27).

Though Peter denied Jesus, and the rest of the apostles, except St. John, abandoned Jesus during his passion (see Matthew 26:56; Mark 14:50), he still chose them to be the foundation of the Church. After his crucifixion and death, they were all in hiding, for fear of the Jewish and Roman authorities. They surely felt shame and guilt for having left Jesus in his time of need. So when Jesus appeared to them after the Resurrection, his words must have been particularly comforting to them: "Peace be with you. As the Father has sent me, even so I send you" (John 20:21).

So I told the man at the bar, "The Bible makes one thing clear about the apostles—they were broken and sinful men. But, despite their brokenness, they went on to become saints. Why? Because Jesus chose to remain in communion with them, despite their faults, and they chose to abide in their relationship with Jesus. They became the foundation of the Church as its first leaders, empowered by Jesus himself to teach in his name. So it follows that members of the Church today have the same potential to become holy by remaining in communion with Jesus despite our brokenness, imperfections, and corruption."

Upon hearing these words, the man's demeanor completely changed. He went from being confrontational to relaxed. I then asked him, "May I ask you a favor?" Seemingly confused, he said, "Sure." I asked, "Will you pray for me, asking for Jesus to transform my corrupt heart into a saintly heart?" Still somewhat confused, he looked at me and then nodded. "Yes," he said.

THE CHURCH ... HOLY OR SINFUL ... OR BOTH?

Every Sunday, Catholics proclaim belief in the "one, holy, catholic, and apostolic Church" when we say the Nicene Creed. In my relatively short time as a priest, I have come to see that most young adults have no problem with the Church professing to be "one," "catholic," or "apostolic" (to the extent that they understand what these terms mean). But *many* of them struggle with the idea that the Church is "holy," given the very public sins of priests, religious, and laity in recent years—and over the past two millennia of the Church's history.

The *Catechism of the Catholic Church* reminds us that all members of the Church, including her ministers, must acknowledge that they are sinners (see CCC 229). During the same Mass we profess that the Church is "holy" during the Creed, we also proclaim the following in the *Confiteor* ("I Confess"):

> *I confess, to almighty God and to you, my brothers and sisters, that I have greatly sinned, in my thoughts and in my words, in what I have done and in what I have failed to do, through my fault, through my fault, through my most grievous fault; therefore I ask blessed Mary ever-Virgin, all the Angels and Saints, and you, my brothers and sisters, to pray for me to the Lord our God.*

So which is it? Are we a "holy" Church? Or a "sinful" Church? The correct answers is "both." The Church is holy, while its members are sinners striving (hopefully) to be saints.

But how can the Church be holy if it is made up of sinners? The Church is holy because of her origin—Jesus Christ. Since the Church was founded by Jesus himself, it must be holy because he is holy and his teachings are holy. In a YouTube video, a young Catholic priest asks Alexa, the digital information device, who founded the various Christian denominations. Alexa reveals that the Lutheran Church was founded by Martin Luther, the Mormon Church by Joseph Smith, and the Methodist Church by John Wesley, among others. Then, the priest asks, "Alexa, who founded the Catholic Church?" Alexa responds, "The Catholic Church was founded by Jesus."

THE CHURCH AND THE BIBLE ...
A MATCH MADE IN HEAVEN

The English word *catholic* is derived from the Greek *katholicos*, which means "according to the whole" or "universal." The Church is the recipient of the fullness of the teachings of Jesus that he passed on to his apostles. In his letter to the Ephesians, St. Paul reveals that Jesus Christ, our cornerstone, built his foundation on the apostles (see Ephesians 2:20). In the first centuries of the Church, if a Christian had a question about how to grow in his or her relationship with God, he or she couldn't simply pick up a copy of the Bible to get an answer. Why? Because the Bible as we now know it did not yet exist!

While several Old Testament books were recognized as divinely inspired by the majority of Jews, there was no official Church "canon" (or approved list) of Scripture until the fourth century AD. So when Christians had questions about their faith, they turned to the apostles and their successors—that is, to the Church—for answers. Though the letters of St. Paul and various gospels were being circulated in the first century, there was yet no determination by the Church as to which were infallibly inspired by the Holy Spirit and which were not. This would take some time and discernment by the Church's bishops.

Early in the fourth century, the bishop and historian Eusebius proposed that the only Christian writings that were divinely inspired were the four Gospels and the letters of St. Paul, as well as the letters of 1 John and 1 Peter.[1] Midway through the fourth century, St. Hilary of Poitiers proposed that the Old Testament books of Tobit and Judith were inspired by the Holy Spirit, but the books of Wisdom, Sirach, 1 and 2 Maccabees, and a portion of Baruch were not. Given all the different opinions over the inspiration of particular books, Pope Damascus called together

---

[1]   Nathan Eubank, *On the Margins of the Developing Canon*, Psalms and Wisdom Literature, Notre Dame Seminary, Received 31 March 2016. Course handout.

a meeting of bishops in AD 382. This meeting, the Synod of Rome, ultimately declared the first "canon" of Scripture. This is the same canon of the Bible the Catholic Church continues to uphold.

Then, in the year 393, the bishops of North Africa met at the Synod of Hippo and affirmed the canon of Scripture that was determined at the Synod of Rome a decade earlier. They convened again at the Synod of Carthage four years later, once again affirming the same collection of biblical books. Finally, the Catholic canon of seventy-three books was affirmed at the Councils of Florence in 1442 and Trent in 1546, the same collection of books that Pope Damascus declared were inspired by the Holy Spirit in the year 382.

Since the Church is described by St. Paul as the "pillar and foundation of faith" (1 Timothy 3:15), it makes sense that the Church determined the canon of Scripture. Jesus gave his apostles the authority to "bind and loose" (Matthew 18:18), and he entrusted them with the authority to choose their successors who would share in their authority through the laying on of hands (see Acts 1:20).

PAUL'S ENCOUNTER WITH JESUS

Jesus not only established the Church on the foundation of the apostles, he also identified himself with the Church. In the Acts of the Apostles, we read how the first Christians were being murdered for their relationship with Christ. One of the chief persecutors of the early Church was a Jewish leader named Saul (later known as St. Paul). As Acts relates, "Saul laid waste the church, and entering house after house, he dragged off men and women and committed them to prison" (Acts 8:3). The fear of Saul among Christians of the first century was akin to the fear European Jews had toward the Nazis in the 1930s and 1940s.

As Saul continued his rampage of murder against the Church, something completely unexpected happened:

> But Saul, still breathing threats and murder against the disciples of the Lord, went to the high priest and asked him for letters to the synagogues at Damascus, so that if he found any belonging to the Way, men or women, he might bring them bound to Jerusalem. Now as he journeyed he approached Damascus, and suddenly a light from heaven flashed about him. And he fell to the ground and heard a voice saying to him, "Saul, Saul, why do you persecute me?" And he said, "Who are you, Lord?" And he said, "I am Jesus, whom you are persecuting" (Acts 9:1-5).

Note that when questioning Saul, Jesus did not ask him, "Why are you persecuting the Christians?" Nor did he ask, "Why are you persecuting the Church?" Rather, Jesus asked, "Why are you persecuting *me*?" (Acts 9:4). Here, then, Jesus directly identified himself with the Christians Saul was persecuting—that is, with the Church.

THE CHURCH AS JESUS' "BRIDE"

Why does Jesus identify himself with the Church, one might ask? Because Jesus is "married" to his Church. Just as in marriage, a man and woman are joined together and become "one flesh," Jesus, the divine Bridegroom (see Matthew 9:5; Mark 2:19; and Luke 5:34) joins himself with the Church, his Bride. This profound truth was proclaimed by Saul after his conversion to Jesus.

In his letter to the church at Ephesus, St. Paul exhorts husbands to love their wives in imitation of the love that Jesus has for the Church (see Ephesians 5:25), who "gave himself up for her." Notice that in this passage he refers to the Church as "her" not as "it" because the Church is Jesus' "Bride." As Paul teaches, Jesus desires to "present the Church to himself in splendor, without wrinkle or any such thing, that she might be holy and without blemish" (Ephesians 5:26-27)—in other words, to make the Church holy. How does he accomplish this? By dying on the Cross.[2]

As St. Augustine wrote in the fourth century:

> Like a bridegroom Christ went forth from his nuptial chamber ... he came even to the marriage-bed of the Cross, and there, ascending it, he consummated a marriage. And when he sensed the creature sighing in her breath, he surrendered himself to torment for his bride in a communication of love.[3]

BROKEN YET HOLY

Despite the brokenness of her individual members, the Church remains holy because she is eternally joined to her Bridegroom, Jesus. The two have become one flesh. So we really cannot think about Jesus without thinking about the Church, and we cannot think about the Church without thinking about Jesus. As the *Catechism* puts it:

> Because Christ, the Son of God, who with the Father and the Spirit is hailed as "alone holy," loved the Church as his Bride, giving himself up for her so as to sanctify her; he joined her to himself as his body and endowed her with the gift of the Holy Spirit for the glory of God." The Church, then, is "the holy People of God," and her members are called "saints" (CCC 823).

The Church, then, is holy not because of anything her members have done, but because of what Jesus did on the Cross two thousand years ago ... and continues to do today through her.

But what about the sins that members of the Catholic Church have committed against humanity? What about the sex scandals of the

---

[2]   Christopher West, *Good News About Sex & Marriage: Answers to Your Honest Questions About Catholic Teaching* (Cincinnati: St. Anthony's Messenger), 21.

[3]   St. Augustine, *Sermo Suppositus,* 120:3.

clergy? What about the religious orders who owned slaves? What about the laity who killed people of different faiths in the name of the Church?

The reality is this: Jesus came to die for sinners. He died for *everyone*, including the sinful members his Church. As has so eloquently been said, "The Church is not a museum of saints but a hospital for sinners." When we are seriously ill, we go to the hospital for treatment and healing. Typically, this healing does not happen overnight. Similarly, Jesus wants to heal us spiritually and morally through his Church, a process that involves our changing our ways, being converted, and growing in our relationship with God.

Reflecting on the vocation of monks, Fr. Reginald Garrigou-Lagrange writes:

> Whenever persons see each other from morning to night throughout the years, in the most varied states of mind and conditions—in sickness and in health, in pain and in joy—one cannot help but notice that together with his many virtues, his confrere also carries some true moral infirmities. A monastery is not yet heaven; it is only the novitiate of heaven, a school of perfection. Even if all the defects would disappear, the occasions for bruises and little conflicts would still exists because of the diversity of feeling, character, education, and because of nervous tensions that derived from such an intense life.[4]

SOLIDARITY WITH (OTHER) SINNERS

With the help of other sinful men and women who are striving to be holy, you and I should be filled with hope. In Jesus and through the ministry of his Church, we are all accompanying each other on our journey to eternal life.

---

[4] Reginald Garrigou-Lagrance, *Knowing the Love of God: Lessons From a Spiritual Master* (DeKalb, Illinois: Lighthouse Catholic Media, 2015), 58.

Being in solidarity with other sinners is what drew acclaimed author G.K. Chesterton to the Catholic Church. As Dr. Tom Neal, a professor at Notre Dame Seminary, writes:

> G.K. Chesterton once said that his umbrella helped reveal to him why he knew the Catholic Church was for him. He said that whenever he went to the non-Catholic churches, he would customarily leave his umbrella by the back door during the worship service. In these churches, his umbrella would always be there waiting for him when he went out back. But the first time he went into a Catholic Church to hear Mass, his umbrella disappeared from the back of the church. Someone had stolen it. His conclusion? If the Catholic Church offered such a generous and open doorway to the rabble, being a home for both sinners and saints, then he had indeed found a home where he could also fumble along into the Kingdom.[5]

St. John Paul II began his pontificate by exclaiming, "Do not be afraid! Open wide the doors of your hearts to the redemptive love of Christ!" (Address of October 27, 1978). Through this book, my desire is to open my heart to you, the reader, in hopes that you will be able to encounter the love of God and his holy and sinful Church in a new way. Though I am a broken and imperfect Christian man and priest, my desire is to accompany you in your journey with Jesus Christ in this life through his Church—with the goal of living together with him in the kingdom of heaven forever.

---

[5]   Tom Neal, "The Church Where Your Umbrella Gets Stolen," Word on Fire Blog. https://www.wordonfire.org/resources/blog/the-church-where-your-umbrella-gets-stolen/5206/ (accessed March 1, 2018).

Invitation to PRAYER

St. Teresa of Calcutta (Mother Teresa) had a well-known devotion to the words of Jesus on the Cross, "I Thirst." Based on these profound words, the Missionaries of Charity Fathers wrote the following meditation:

"Behold, I stand at the door and knock" (Revelation 3:20).

It is true. I stand at the door of your heart, day and night. Even when you are not listening, even when you doubt it could be me, I am there. I await even the smallest sign of your response, even the least whispered invitation that will allow me to enter.

And I want you to know that whenever you invite me, I do come always without fail. Silent and unseen I come, but with infinite power and love, and bringing the many gifts of my spirit. I come with my mercy, with my desire to forgive and heal you, and with a love for you beyond your comprehension—a love every bit as great as the love I have received from the Father, ("As much as the Father has loved me, I have loved you ..." [John 15:9]). I come—longing to console you and give you strength, to lift you up and bind all your wounds. I bring you my light, to dispel your darkness and all your doubts. I come with my power, that I might carry you and all of your burdens; with my grace, to touch your heart and transform your life; and my peace I give to still your soul.

I know you through and through—I know everything about you. The very hairs of your head I have numbered. Nothing in your life is unimportant to me. I have followed you through the years, and I have always loved you—even in your wanderings. I know everyone of your problems. I know your needs and your worries. And yes, I know all your sins. But I tell you again that I love you—not for what you have or haven't done—I love you for you, for the beauty and dignity my Father gave you by creating you in his own image. It is a dignity you have often forgotten, a beauty you have tarnished by sin. But I love you as you are, and I have shed my blood to win you back. If you only ask me with faith, my grace will touch all that needs changing in your life; and I will give you the strength to free yourself from sin and all its destructive power.

I know what is in your heart. I know your loneliness and all your hurts—the rejections, the judgments, the humiliations. I carried it all before you. And I carried it all for you, so you might share my strength and victory. I know especially your need for love—how you are thirsting to be loved and cherished. But how often have you thirsted in vain, by seeking that love selfishly, striving to fill the emptiness inside you with passing pleasures, with the even greater emptiness of sin. Do you thirst for love? "Come to me all of you who thirst …" (John 7:37). I will satisfy you and fill you. Do you thirst to be cherished? I cherish you more than you can imagine—to the point of dying on a cross for you.

I thirst for you. Yes, that is the only way to even begin to describe my love for you: I THIRST FOR YOU. I thirst to love you and to be loved by you—that is how precious you are to me. I THIRST FOR YOU. Come to me and I will fill your heart and heal your wounds. I will make you a new creation and give you peace, even in all your trials. I THIRST FOR YOU. You must never doubt my mercy, my acceptance of you, my desire to forgive, my longing to bless you and live my life in you. I THIRST FOR YOU. If you feel unimportant in the eyes of the world, that matters not at all. For me, there is no one any more important in the entire world than you. I THIRST FOR YOU.

Open to me, come to me, thirst for me, give me your life—and I will prove to you how important you are to my Heart.

Don't you realize that my Father already has a perfect plan to transform your life, beginning from this moment? Trust in me. Ask me every day to enter and take charge of your life—and I will. I promise you before my father in heaven that I will work miracles in your life. Why would I do this? Because I THIRST FOR YOU. All I ask of you is that you entrust yourself to me completely. I will do all the rest.

Even now, I behold the place my Father has prepared for you in my kingdom. Remember that you are a pilgrim in this life, on a journey home. Sin can never satisfy you or bring the peace you seek. All that you have sought outside of me has only left you more empty, so do not cling to the things of this life. Above all, do not run from me when you fall. Come to me without delay. When you give me your sins, you give me the joy of being your Savior. There is nothing I cannot forgive and heal, so come now and unburden your soul.

No matter how far you may wander, no matter how often you forget me, no matter how many crosses you may bear in this life, there is one thing I want you to always remember, one thing that will never change: I THIRST FOR YOU, just as you are. You don't need to change to believe in my love, for it will be your belief in my love that will change you. You forget me, and yet I am seeking you every moment of the day, standing at the door of your heart and knocking. Do you find this hard to believe? Then look at the cross, look at my Heart that was pierced for you. Have you not understood my cross? Then listen again to the words I spoke there—for they tell you clearly why I endured all this for you: "I THIRST ..." (John 19:20). Yes, I thirst for you—as the rest of the psalm-verses I was praying says of me: "I looked for love, and I found none ..."

(Psalm 69:20). All your life I have been looking for your love. I have never stopped seeking to love you and be loved by you. You have tried many other things in your search for happiness; why not try opening your heart to me, right now, more than you ever have before.

Whenever you do open the door of your heart, whenever you come close enough, you will hear me say to you again and again, not in mere human words but in spirit: "No matter what you have done, I love you for your own sake. Come to me with your misery and your sins, with your troubles and needs, and with all your longing to be loved. I stand at the door of your heart and knock ... open to ME, for I THIRST FOR YOU ..."

"Jesus is God, therefore his love, his thirst is infinite. He, the creator of the universe, asked for the love of his creatures. He thirsts for our love ... these words: I THIRST ... do they echo in our souls?" (St. Teresa of Calcutta).

QUESTIONS
For Meditation and Discussion

1. Does any part of Jesus choosing his apostles speak to you? Do you feel like you are one of Jesus' chosen ones? Do you feel challenged to bring this message to others?

2. If you have not perceived Jesus calling you, what might be holding you back from hearing his voice? How can you be more open to being one of Jesus' chosen ones?

3. Do you believe the Bible was inspired by the Holy Spirit? How can the Bible help you on your journey to encountering Jesus?

4. Can you truly embrace your role as a sinful member of the body of Christ, walking in solidarity with other sinners in Jesus? How might you be able to do this more deeply?

5. Can you imagine Christ "thirsting" for you? Who (or what) do you thirst for? Can you imagine God's love satisfying all you thirst for?

Chapter Two

Come, Follow Me

On a beautiful spring day in May of 2013, I was ordained to the transitional diaconate, which is the final step toward being ordained a priest. Two days later, I eagerly began my assignment at St. Patrick's Catholic Church in Baton Rouge, Louisiana. One of the first tasks the pastor assigned me was to teach religious education to tenth graders. So I walked into a classroom of twenty students and, with enthusiasm, asked them, "How many of y'all want to be saints?" Immediately followed thirty seconds or so of surprised silence, as the teens looked at each other, confused. They were trying to figure out whether this was some sort of trick question.

Finally, after this brief, awkward pause—which seemed to last an eternity—two students timidly raised their hands. I was a bit taken aback by their reluctance. In my newly ordained exuberance, I thought my question would evoke unanimous high fives and cheers. Feeling like a standup comic whose material is bombing with his audience, I decided to rephrase the question: "OK, apparently not too many of you want to be saints. So my next question is, 'How many of y'all want to go to hell?'" This time, the silence was replaced by an audible gasp, followed by loud declarations of their intention to avoid that prospect. This made me smile. I then went on to remind them that each would either end up as a saint in heaven (after being purified by God's grace, either here on earth or in purgatory) or as an unrepentant sinner in hell—forever, no less. I then asked them one more time, "So, now, how many of y'all want to be saints in heaven for all eternity?" They all responded with a resounding, "I do!"

A UNIVERSAL CALL

I often wonder why so many people resist the call of Jesus to become saints, which is nothing more than a call to live a holy life. Many seem to have gotten the idea that the only saints are those canonized by the Church. But God calls each and every one of us to be saints. The Church refers to this as the "universal call to holiness," which St. Paul writes about in his first letter to Timothy: "This is good, and it is acceptable in the sight of God our Savior, who desires all men to be saved and to come to knowledge of the truth" (1 Timothy 2:3-4).

If God calls every human being to be in a relationship with him, why are we so reserved in our response to this invitation? In his book *The Fulfillment of All Desire,* Dr. Ralph Martin offers an answer to this perplexing question:

> We all probably know in some way that we are called to holiness but perhaps struggle to respond. Feeling the challenge of the call and yet seeing the obstacles, it is easy to rationalize delaying or compromising and avoid a wholehearted and immediate response.
>
> It is not uncommon, for example, to "pass the buck" to others whom we deem in a better position to respond wholeheartedly. Those of us who are Catholic lay people often look at our busy lives and sluggish hearts and suppose that priests and nuns are in a better position to respond to the call. After all, we may

think to ourselves, that's what we pay them for! We may think that when our kids are grown, or when we retire, or after a business crisis passes, or when we don't have to care for ailing parents, or when we get a better job, or when we get married … that then we will be in a better position to respond.[1]

FEARS OF REJECTION … AND UNWORTHINESS

So what it is it? Why do we resist the invitation to be in relationship with Jesus and the Church? In all honesty, there are probably *hundreds* of reasons. Based on my relatively limited experience as a priest, I think two of the most common reasons are a fear of rejection and a sense of being unworthy of such a call. In the tenth-grade religious education class I mentioned earlier, the two students who timidly raised their hands only did so half-heartedly—and they quickly put them down when they realized that they were the only ones who had them up. Like nearly all of us, they were concerned with fitting in. They certainly did not want to be rejected by their classmates for standing out or being different.

Of course, a fear of rejection is not limited to teenagers. Some years ago, I was driving through Baton Rouge with a friend who was also notorious locally as a gangster rapper and a drug dealer. Though he had been raised Catholic, he had not been to Church in many years. As we were driving, I challenged him, "Why don't you come back to church?" He responded, "You know I can't do that. I sell drugs! I sleep with a different woman every night. And I don't plan on changing my lifestyle. I would be a hypocrite if I came back to church. I don't belong there. God and the people who go to church don't want people like me around them." As he spoke, I began to pray silently. In that silent prayer, I remembered something a youth minister said at a conference years earlier about God's transformative love.

---

[1] Ralph Martin, *The Fulfillment of All Desire: A Guidebook for the Journey to God Based on the Wisdom of the Saints* (Steubenville, OH: Emmaus Road Publishing, 2006), 6-7.

"Can I ask you a question?"

"Sure," he said.

I then invited him to imagine the following scenario:

"You get home after a long day's work, and you are planning to go out with one of your girlfriends. You are dirty and sweaty from working outside all day, so you decide to get cleaned up before your date. You have two options:

1. You can try to get clean by scrubbing the dirt and sweat off of your body before jumping in the shower. Or,

2. You can jump in the shower right away—all dirty and sweaty—and allow the soap and water of the shower to cleanse you.

Which option makes the most sense?"

He replied, "Obviously, jumping in the shower right away, all dirty and sweaty, and let it do its work."

"Right!" I said. "And that is the same way God cleanses us spiritually."

NO "SPIRITUAL MAKEOVERS" REQUIRED

I went on to explain that God does not want us to "get our lives together" before we seek an intentional relationship with him—and his Church. The beauty of God's love is that he truly meets us where we are, no matter how "dirty" or "unclean" we might be. We do not have to go through a "spiritual makeover" before we meet God; we do not need to present "before" and "after" pictures. Perfection is not required to walk with God and each other.

The famous Irish poet and playwright Oscar Wilde once remarked that "every saint has a past, and every sinner has a future." The mistakes of our past should not dictate our future; they need not keep us from becoming saints. If we allow it, God's grace will perfect us over time. Just as we enter a shower dirty and allow it to cleanse us, Christ wants to do the same. If we come to church as we are, broken, imperfect, corrupt, and sinful, then we will give God the opportunity to transform us. But if we never show up or seek to have a relationship with Jesus, he will not force himself on us. God never imposes … he only invites.

Just as my friend feared rejection from God and the Church because of his sinfulness, St. Peter, the first pope, was also acutely aware of his sins and weaknesses. He, too, assumed that Jesus would not want him to be an apostle because of his imperfections. As St. Luke recounts:

> While the people pressed upon him to hear the word of God, he was standing by the lake of Gennesaret. And he saw two boats by the lake; but the fishermen had gone out of them and were washing their nets. Getting into one of the boats, which was Simon's, he asked him to put out a little from the land. And he sat down and taught the people from the boat. And when he had ceased speaking, he said to Simon, "Put out into the deep and let down your nets for a catch." And Simon answered, "Master, we toiled all night and took nothing! But at your word I will let down the nets." And when they had done this, they enclosed a great shoal of fish; and as their nets were breaking, they beckoned to their partners in the other boat to come and help them. And they came and filled both the boats, so that they began to sink. But when Simon Peter saw it, he fell down at Jesus' knees, saying, "Depart from me, for I am a sinful man, O Lord." For he was astonished, and all that were with him, at the catch of fish which they had taken; and so also were James and John, sons of Zebedee, who were partners with Simon. And Jesus said to Simon, "Do not

be afraid; henceforth you will be catching men." And when
they had brought their boats to land, they left everything and
followed him (Luke 5:1-11).

St. Peter witnessed one of the first miracles of Jesus. So he
knew there was something special about this carpenter from
Nazareth. But Peter's response to Jesus in this fishing episode
is very interesting: "Depart from me, for I am a sinful man." In
the presence of the all-holy Son of God, Peter becomes acutely
aware of his sinfulness. What were Peter's particular sins up to
that moment in his life? We don't know; the Bible doesn't tells us.
It really isn't important. The point here is that we can all relate to
his feelings of unworthiness before God.

As the *Catechism of the Catholic Church* teaches regarding Peter's
first encounter with Jesus:

> Faced with God's fascinating and mysterious presence, man
> discovers his own insignificance ... Before the divine signs
> wrought by Jesus, Peter exclaims: "Depart from me, for I am a
> sinful man, O Lord." But because God is holy, he can forgive
> the man who realizes that he is a sinner before him ... The
> apostle John says likewise: "We shall ... reassure our hearts
> before him whenever our hearts condemn us; for God is
> greater than our hearts, and he knows everything" (CCC 208).

It is natural if our response to the presence of holiness is to focus on
our sin, our imperfections and failings. But God, who knows us better
than we know ourselves, sees things quite differently—he sees our
potential. He sees beyond the present moment to the "big picture" of
our existence. In the episode on the boat, Jesus sees beyond Peter's
feelings of unworthiness to his future ministry as an apostle—how
he will enter into the sinfulness of his brothers and sisters in Christ
and bring them God's saving truth and mercy.

FEAR OF REJECTION AND PEER PRESSURE:
A DANGEROUS COMBINATION

Similarly to St. Peter, I allowed my fear of rejection to navigate my relationship with God and the Church for many years. I grew up as the youngest of seven children who were blessed to have devoted, loving parents. But my parents' devotion to each other and to their children had its challenges. You see, my father is an African-American and my mom Caucasian. Even in the 1980s, when I was born, most people in the South disapproved of mixed-race couples, and this disapproval was sometimes subtle but sometimes not. Fortunately, my parents' strong bond of love and faith enabled them to persevere in their life together as a family. Though he had been raised Protestant, my father agreed with my Catholic mother to raise us in the Church.

Our parish was predominantly white, but there were a few black parishioners as well. There were even a few biracial families. Perhaps not surprisingly, most of the white parishioners were not too interested in having a relationship with our family. Any feeling of inclusion we had in the parish was limited to other minority families. Even as a young child, I remember sensing the rejection of the majority toward us—and I knew I did not like that feeling. Looking back on those days, I know that I was not alone in this feeling, as my brothers and I began to seek community elsewhere—at school, in sports, and in music. At home, we prayed to God as a family, but to me, the God we prayed to seemed impersonal, remote, no doubt a reflection of the lack of community we experienced in our parish.

Down the street from our home was a neighborhood park and gym. My brothers and I spent most of our adolescence there. I formed some of my first friendships at this gym. When I played basketball with my brothers and our neighborhood friends there, I felt accepted—and I knew that I liked that feeling.

When I was eight, one of my friends invited me to sleep over at his house. We ended up staying up late talking about all the things that occupy the imaginations of eight-year-old boys: things like who would win out of a fight between Superman and Batman, which wrestler on television had the best finisher—Steve Austin's "Stone Cold Stunner" or Dwayne Johnson's "Rock Bottom"—and who was the best player on the USA Dream Team. (To be honest, I still have these types of conversations today!)

That night, as my friend and I sorted out all of the main problems of the world, something happened that changed the course of my life. He asked if I could keep a secret. "Sure," I said, excited about what he was going to tell me. Then, we went into his older brother's room and opened his brother's bottom dresser drawer. He pulled out a magazine that my young eyes were not prepared to see, a pornographic magazine, a magazine in which women were being portrayed as sexual objects.

I immediately knew that this was something I should not be looking at. But I knew well the feeling of rejection, and I was afraid that if I said something, he might not want to be my friend anymore. Every time we looked at those pictures, I knew in my heart it was wrong, but I would rather be wrong than be rejected.

As I grew older, especially as I entered adolescence, I began to objectify the girls in my school. There's an old saying: "We are called to love people and use things." Unfortunately, by objectifying the girls in my life, I was using people as things. Even as a fourth grader, I began pursuing relationships with girls. I certainly did not love them—at that age, I had no idea how to love them. I simply wanted to use them; the images I had been exposed to had trained me to think of them as objects rather than as people. Regrettably, this disordered way of thinking and living would continue throughout middle school and high school.

As I entered my teen years, a new temptation was placed in front of me: alcohol and illegal drugs. Though some of my friends drank alcohol at parties and occasionally used drugs, I never thought I would fall into these vices. Initially, they just weren't that enticing to me. I vividly remembered a D.A.R.E. (Drug Abuse Resistance Education) presentation in sixth grade when we were told the story of a young teenager who died the very first time he smoked marijuana. I was shocked. *Nope,* I thought. *Not me.* I would never smoke weed or take drugs.

I kept this promise until one night when I was hanging out with a bunch of guys playing basketball. A few of them were smoking weed, and they offered me some. But I passed, saying I was OK just hanging out and shooting hoops. At the time, my best friend and I were still able to fit in without using drugs. Soon, though, my best friend gave in to peer pressure and began to smoke weed with them. I was now all alone in my sobriety. For three years, I continued to be invited to play with them without giving in. But the pressure to join in became overwhelming, and I gave in. I felt terrible, but the fear of rejection trumped any regrets I had at the time.

As I began high school, God was nowhere on my radar. Every Sunday morning, I acted like the main character in the movie *Ferris Bueller's Day Off,* faking stomachaches that began when we got dressed for Mass and ended as soon as my family went out the door without me. Basically, my relationship with God was nonexistent. Socially, however, I seemed to be thriving. I was dating the girl of my dreams, and I had a best friend with whom I could talk about anything. Life was great—that was, until my girlfriend broke up with me and my best friend moved out of state. I had counted on those relationships, and now they were gone. I couldn't stand the emptiness I felt inside.

No amount of parties, random dates, or sports could satiate the ache I felt in my core. For the first time in my life, I dropped to my knees and I said a prayer to God. I remember it as if it were yesterday. I was in my older brother's dimly lit bedroom, kneeling on the floor with my eyes closed, and these were the words that I prayed: "God, if you are real, please send me some new friends. The people I am currently hanging out with are not really my friends. They don't really care about me. Please send me some real friends … and if you don't mind, please send me a new girlfriend, too!" I then described in detail the kind of girl God should send me. I know that sounds more like a letter to Santa Claus than a prayer, but it was a start!

SOME NEW (CHRISTIAN) FRIENDS

As the next school year began, God answered my prayers. I became close with a group of guys that I had known since middle school and had hung out with occasionally over the years. The time we spent together was very intentional, consistent, and life-giving; I didn't feel pressured to do anything that I knew was not good for me. I also began to date a girl I had met at a party. She was very different from any other girl I had dated in the past. All the others were mainly concerned with themselves, but she was focused on serving her family and classmates.

As awesome as these new relationships were, I was uncomfortable with one aspect of this new season of my life. My new friends were Christians; they all loved Jesus and had a personal relationship with him. Though my parents forced us to attend Mass and religious education classes, I had no desire to have a relationship with Jesus. After spending most weekends with them, my Christian friends invited me to join them at an upcoming Protestant youth conference called "Acquire the Fire." At the time, I thought that this was the least attractive invitation I had ever received. I literally had no desire to attend this conference. Once again, though, my fear of rejection came back, and I heard a little voice in my head: *If you don't go to this conference, then your new friends—who you really enjoy hanging out with—might not want to be your friends anymore.*

So I went to the Acquire the Fire conference—not because I was at all open to encountering Jesus, but simply because I wanted to be with my friends. In some ways, this was like Jesus' parable of the Prodigal Son, who decided to go back home to his father after spending his entire inheritance on passing pleasures (see Luke 15:11-32). He went home not because he was sorry for his sins against his father (and God, for that matter), but only because he was hungry, and he knew he could get a good meal at home. Similarly, I only went to the conference because I didn't want to lose my friends.

What I encountered at this conference was shocking. I witnessed thousands of teenagers jumping up and down as they praised God from the top of their lungs, and I heard powerful testimonies from speakers about their faith in Jesus, as well as some great worship and praise music. On the last night of the conference, the pastor invited everyone who had not given his or her life to Jesus to come to the stage to pray with him and be saved. This is what is called an "altar call" in some Protestant Christian communities. One by one, each of my friends stood up and walked to the stage. I felt a wave of emotions as I, too, felt the urge to "try a relationship with Jesus" out. I stood up, and I followed my friends. I gave my life to Jesus.

Shortly after returning home from Acquire the Fire, I had a conversation with my girlfriend, who was a Baptist. I told her about my experience at the conference. She listened attentively and then asked me a question I was not expecting: "Now that you have given your life to Jesus, do you still consider yourself a Catholic?" I said, "Yeah, I guess so. Why?" She responded by saying that Catholics were not Christians, claiming that Catholics worship the Virgin Mary and statues and believe many other things that are not "biblical." Now that I had given my life to Jesus and become a "true" Christian, she said, I could no longer be Catholic.

At the time, I was very ignorant about my Catholic faith, so I accepted her views. As I look back on these conversations, I am humbled by how little I understood the teachings of the Church. It was a lack of understanding that caused me to no longer want to be affiliated with the Catholic Church in any way.

With my girlfriend's encouragement, I began attending non-denominational Christian services on Thursday and Saturday nights and on Sundays. (Since I was no longer going to Mass with my family, I told my mother that I was attending with a friend. I never went, of course.) My level of faith and my relationship with Christ, though, remained superficial at best. For example, I did not spend any intentional or consistent time in prayer. My fears of rejection were still dominating my perspective.

As a result, I compartmentalized my relationships. I hung out with my "pre-Jesus" friends a few nights a week, doing things that were contrary to what I now believed, things that left me feeling empty inside. The other nights, I would hang out with my Jesus-centered friends, participating in Bible study, singing praise and worship songs, and assisting with the weekly "altar calls." But I was unhappy.

I couldn't figure it out. What was missing? From all appearances, my life was pretty good. I had a solid group of friends, and I had a wonderful, beautiful girlfriend. Nonetheless, I had a consistently inconsistent relationship with Jesus—which I naively justified. Surely, that couldn't possibly be the "missing piece." So what was it that continued to make my heart feel so empty and heavy?

CONFIRMATION AND CRISIS

As I was experiencing this existential crisis, the sacrament of confirmation was fast approaching. I remembered my older brothers' responses to being confirmed: They immediately stopped setting foot in a Catholic Church. For them, confirmation was like "graduating" from the Church. I had no understanding that confirmation was about receiving an outpouring of the gifts of the Holy Spirit. Since I now believed that the Catholic Church was not in line with the Bible, I actually considered not being confirmed. Providentially, though, I decided to check in with a few Catholics and ask some important questions.

Looking back, I realize that my naiveté was becoming arrogance. In effect, I was inventing my own version of faith that satisfied what I thought I needed at the time. As I spoke with some knowledgeable Catholics, though, and did some reading, I discovered that Catholics do not *worship* Mary; they simply *honor* her as the Mother of God and as our spiritual mother as well. Nor do Catholics worship statues. After all, God himself ordered Moses to create a bronze serpent (see Numbers 21:9) and instructed the construction of the Ark of the Covenant, which had two golden "statues" of angels on top (see Exodus 37).

Though I was relieved to know that my mother, as a practicing Catholic, was not a member of a pagan religion, I still had no intention of remaining Catholic. I decided that I would follow in the spirit of my siblings and treat confirmation as if it were a graduation from the Church. I went through the motions of receiving the sacrament, and I thought that this would be my last day as a Catholic.

As I sipped on red punch at the reception following the ceremony, a young lady from my confirmation class approached me with a huge smile on her face. Though I didn't like much about religion class, I had always been impressed by her. She stood out from the rest. She was joyful and prayerful, and she never missed Mass. She clearly was in love with Jesus. Though white, she went out of her way to spend time with the black students in our class— something none of the others did.

As we drank our glasses of punch, she asked me a question that would change my life. She said, "Would you like to come with me and the youth group to the Steubenville South Youth Conference this summer?" Without thinking, I responded, "Sure, I would love to!"

I immediately came to my senses. *What? Wait a minute! Attend a Catholic youth conference? No!*

Though inwardly reluctant to attend, I had accepted her invitation and wanted to follow through as a "man of my word." As I joined her and our local youth group to head to Alexandria, Louisiana, I didn't realize that I was about to experience a weekend that would change the entire course of my life. Put in digital terms, I was getting ready to follow an entirely new set of GPS coordinates for an entirely new journey—a true relationship with Jesus and his Church for the rest of my life.

The intention of falling in love with Jesus in the depths of my heart was certainly not foremost in my mind as I arrived for the opening night of the Steubenville South Youth Conference. The thousands of young people praising the Lord with a deafening enthusiasm similar to what I had experienced at Acquire the Fire could not drown out the pleas of my heart for something more. That evening, as I looked at all these obviously happy and fulfilled teens, the contrast to my own empty heart shocked me. As the night progressed, I heard heartfelt testimonies from several speakers and uplifting music. But my heart remained only slightly moved.

Providentially, the next day I experienced a *metanoia*, a realization, that was and remains life-changing. As a participant, I followed the schedule of talks and opportunities for prayer and fellowship, with the concluding event being Adoration of the Blessed Sacrament.

RECOGNIZING JESUS IN THE EUCHARIST

The Catholic Church teaches that, during the words of consecration at Mass, the bread and wine of the Holy Eucharist actually becomes the Body, Blood, Soul, and Divinity of Jesus Christ. Adoration is an extended period of prayer with Jesus in the Eucharist. I had always struggled to accept what to me was a traditional symbol of the Catholic Church, ordinary bread meant to evoke Jesus' celebration at the Last Supper. I was familiar with the words of this pivotal moment, but I only later came to understand the significance of Jesus' repeated proclamations—that the Eucharist is his actual Body and Blood, not just a symbol.

In the Gospel of John, Jesus preached to a multitude of his disciples and proclaimed:

> I am the bread of life ... if anyone eats of this bread, he will live forever; and the bread which I shall give for the life of the world is my flesh ... Truly, truly, I say to you, unless you eat the flesh of the Son of man and drink his blood, you have no life in you; he who eats my flesh and drinks my blood has eternal life ... he who eats my flesh and drinks my blood abides in me, and I in him (John 6:35, 51, 53-54).

At the Steubenville conference, I truly recognized Jesus in the Eucharist for the first time in my life. While I had understood intellectually that Eucharistic Adoration is intended to be a period of contemplation of Jesus Christ truly present in the host, I now found myself open to the grace of the Holy Spirit. I felt God drawing himself to me, gently transforming my heart. As I knelt and began to adore Jesus, I realized that he was the One for whom I had been searching to satisfy the aching emptiness in my heart.

This recognition was immediate, as if a spiritual light had suddenly been turned on in the darkness: Jesus was the One who would fulfill my soul's desires and quench its thirst. I realized that, as I thrashed around in all directions and looked for love in all the wrong places, Jesus had been patiently waiting for me in the Eucharist. This was the first glimpse I had of Christ's unconditional and eternal love—for me.

At this moment of spiritual awakening, I asked the Lord Jesus what his will was for my life. Expecting some specific instructions or a life plan, what I perceived were the words "I love you"—not, "I used to love you before you began to live a life of sin," or, "I will love you when you get your life together." Just, "I love you." As St. John tells us, "God is love ... In this is love, not that we loved God but that he loves us" (1 John 4:8, 10).

In the depths of our hearts, we all desire love. Our fear of rejection is usually associated with the desire to love and be loved. Now I realized: Jesus sees me, and he loves me! He did not do what I feared most throughout my life: He did not reject me!

As Jesus tells us, "Come to me, all of you who labor and are burdened, and I will give you rest" (Matthew 11:28). The moment I perceived the love of Jesus Christ in prayer during Eucharistic Adoration, I knew that I had found my "rest." I did not have to grasp at earthly solutions for my happiness; it would come from God alone. I was loved by God, and I was in love with God. My ache was satiated, my thirst was quenched, and my desires were fulfilled by the love of God in the Eucharist. I knew that this love would be the compass, my navigation source, for the rest of my life.

As I prayed in gratitude for my newfound understanding of God's intimate love, it began to dawn on me—like the lifting of a thick curtain blocking a beautiful view—that Jesus was offering me a direction to follow in my life. I began to sense that he was asking me to discern a vocation to the priesthood. I was taken aback, because I had never seen a black Catholic priest. I knew that they had to exist, but I had never met one. And here I was, actually considering a priestly vocation!

A few months after Steubenville, I was invited to another Catholic youth conference at which the keynote speaker was a Franciscan priest from the Bronx, Fr. Stan Fortuna. He had a very atypical look, with the coolest braids all the way down his back. Turns out, he was a priest *and* a rapper. I was in awe. For the first time in my life, here was a priest to whom I could relate. Given his dark complexion, I assumed he was biracial; turns out, he was just Italian! During Mass, Fr. Fortuna left the sanctuary and walked directly to me to offer the sign of peace. Curiously, he did not do this with anyone else, including his brother priests. Though I didn't know what to think, this experience was a "game-changer." I was inspired to reach out to the vocations director of my diocese.

The more time I spent in Eucharistic Adoration actively discerning the priesthood, the more I fell in love with Jesus. The love for Jesus I felt in prayer fulfilled all my desires; it was beyond my imagination. After several years of spending consistent time with Jesus, I responded to his invitation to enter the seminary and discern if he was indeed calling me to be a priest.

Dwelling on our fear of rejection can paralyze us in our lives, especially in our walk with God. When we choose instead to focus on Jesus' unconditional love for each of us, despite our brokenness, we can respond with joy to his invitation: "Come, follow me."

Invitation to PRAYER

As we begin to experience the love of God, the following prayer can be a powerful tool in dispelling our doubts and fears.

From the belief that I have to earn your love …
Deliver me, Jesus.

From the fear that I am unlovable …
Deliver me, Jesus.

From the false security that I have what it takes …
Deliver me, Jesus.

From the fear that trusting you will leave me more destitute …
Deliver me, Jesus.

From all suspicion of your words and promises …
Deliver me, Jesus.

From the rebellion against childlike dependency on you …
Deliver me, Jesus.

From refusals and reluctances in accepting your will …
Deliver me, Jesus.

From anxiety about the future …
Deliver me, Jesus.

From resentment or excessive preoccupation with the past …
Deliver me, Jesus.

From restless self-seeking in the present moment …
Deliver me, Jesus.

From disbelief in your love and presence …
Deliver me, Jesus.

From the fear of being asked to give more than I have …
Deliver me, Jesus.

From the belief that my life has no meaning or worth …
Deliver me, Jesus.

From the fear of what love demands …
Deliver me, Jesus.

From discouragement …
Deliver me, Jesus.

That you are continually holding me, sustaining me, loving me …
Jesus, I trust in you.

*That your love goes deeper than my sins and failings and
    transforms me …*
Jesus, I trust in you.

*That not knowing what tomorrow brings is an invitation to
    lean on you …*
Jesus, I trust in you.

That you are with me in my suffering …
Jesus, I trust in you.

*That my suffering, united to your own, will bear fruit in this
    life and the next …*
Jesus, I trust in you.

*That you will not leave me orphan, that you are present in
    your Church …*
Jesus, I trust in you.

That your plan is better than anything else …
Jesus, I trust in you.

*That you always hear me and, in your goodness, always
    respond to me …*
Jesus, I trust in you.

*That you give me the grace to accept forgiveness and to
    forgive others …*
Jesus, I trust in you.

That you give me all the strength I need for what is asked …
Jesus, I trust in you.

That my life is a gift …
Jesus, I trust in you.

That you will teach me to trust you …
Jesus, I trust in you.

That you are my Lord and my God …
Jesus, I trust in you.

That I am your beloved one …
Jesus, I trust in you.

"The Litany of Trust"
by Sister Faustina Maria Pia of the Sisters of Life

QUESTIONS
For Meditation and Discussion

1. Do you truly believe God loves you? Do you believe he wants an intimate and intentional relationship with you? How do you experience God's love for you?

2. All of us have experienced rejection at some point in our lives. How did that make you feel? Are you afraid that God will reject you because of your sins and imperfections?

3. Do you find yourself dwelling on your past, focusing on your mistakes? Are you open to God's mercy and forgiveness (especially in the sacrament of reconciliation)?

4. Do you believe God is calling you to be holy? To be a saint? If not, why do you find this idea difficult to accept?

5. How might the desire to be holy influence your relationships and choices?

6. If you were raised Catholic, were you ever taught that you are called to a personal relationship with Jesus? How might this affect the way you live your faith?

7. Do you surround yourself with people who help you grow closer to God? Or with people who draw you away from him?

8. Since Jesus is truly present in the Eucharist, do you spend any time in Adoration of the Blessed Sacrament? If you do, how has this devotion affected your relationship with Jesus and his Church?

CHAPTER THREE

Who Told You That?

All my life, I have been a creature of habit. Like many people, I have a daily routine—what time I wake up, when I eat breakfast, when I use the restroom, when I pray, etc. If I go to a restaurant, I usually order one of three items every time. Like others, I enjoy the security that my daily routine provides. The idea of "routine" extends to my way of thinking, and changing this perspective can be challenging.

In high school, my girlfriend and I had a routine for date nights. We would meet up, see a movie, and then go to dinner. In 2004, Mel Gibson's highly anticipated film *The Passion of the Christ* hit the theaters around the world and became a global box office smash. As was our custom, my girlfriend and I were headed to the movies that weekend, and we decided to see *The Passion*.

At the box office, the ticket clerk challenged us about our ages. *The Passion* was rated R due to its extreme, realistic violence, and both my girlfriend and I were only sixteen. With typical teenage enthusiasm, we were undeterred by this obstacle and came up with an easy (if morally questionable) solution. We purchased tickets to a PG-13 movie playing in the theater next door and then sneaked into *The Passion of the Christ*. Even then, I was aware of the irony of the situation: We were committing a sin (a venial sin, but a sin nonetheless) to see a film about the Person who died for our sins! (And yes, in case you are wondering, I did later confess this sin of deception in the sacrament of reconciliation.)

As we watched this powerful film, I became quite emotional. Though I had heard the story of Jesus' passion growing up, like many, I never really imagined how much he suffered for me. Seeing the graphic visual images of his suffering touched my heart very deeply. Tears slowly fell down my face, with sniffles following. My girlfriend glanced at me a couple of times. Then the unfathomable happened. At *The Passion's* quietest moment, she loudly gasped, "Awwwww! Are you crying?" Of course, I wanted her to think I was a tough guy, so I blamed my tears on allergies. But the damage had been done. She had publicly embarrassed me.

That embarrassing moment aside, what stuck with me most about *The Passion of the Christ* is its first ten minutes. Using both Scripture and the private revelations of certain mystics, Mel Gibson opens the film with the encounter between Jesus and Satan in the Garden of Gethsemane. The following is based on the translated dialogue of the film:

Jesus, falling to his knees, prays to his Father:

"Hear me, Father. Rise up, defend me. Save me from the traps they set for me."

Satan appears in the background and asks Jesus:

"Do you really believe that one man can bear the full burden of sin?"

Jesus doesn't respond to the devil's question. Instead, he keeps his gaze on the Father and prays:

"Shelter me, O Lord. I trust in you. In you, I take refuge."

Satan continues his challenge:

"No one man can carry this burden, I tell you. It is far too heavy. Saving their souls is too costly. No one. Ever. No. Never."

Again, Jesus keeps his focus on his Father, praying:

"Father, you can do all things. If it is possible, let this cup pass from me. But let your will be done, not mine."

As Jesus falls prostrate on the ground in prayer, Satan leans in closer and asks:

"Who is your father? Who are you?"

Then, the devil releases a snake, which slithers its way under Jesus. The Lord then stands up, looks Satan in the eye, and crushes the snake's head with his foot.

This scene is remarkable for a number of reasons.

1. Jesus is tempted by Satan.

As I began studying theology, one of my biggest "hang-ups" was grasping how Jesus, as a divine Person, could experience temptation. The Bible makes it clear that Jesus was tempted by the devil after his forty days in the desert following his baptism: "The Spirit immediately drove [Jesus] out into the wilderness. And he was in the wilderness for forty days, tempted by Satan" (Mark 1:12-13).

So, just as *The Passion of the Christ* portrays, Scripture affirms that Jesus was tempted by the devil. But how is this possible? Jesus, though possessing a true human nature, is a divine Person and was incarnate without sin. As such, he did not suffer—as we do—from *concupiscence*, which is the tendency to sin we inherited from our first parents. So if he cannot sin, how can he be tempted?

The learned sixth-century pope and theologian St. Gregory the Great addresses this question:

Temptation is brought to fulfillment by three stages: suggestion, delight, and consent. And we in temptation generally fall through delight and then through consent, for being begotten of the sin of the flesh we bear within us that through which we suffer conflict ... But God incarnate ... came into the world without sin and so suffers no conflict within himself. He could therefore be tempted by suggestion, but the delight of sin could never touch his mind. So all these temptations of the devil are *from without, not from within* him.[1]

According to St. Gregory, then, Satan is able to tempt Jesus with "suggestion." These sinful suggestions to Jesus can only be from *outside* of his mind, not from within (as they can be with us). For example, a young lawyer takes his first job right out of law school. He and his wife are expecting their first child. In the firm's break room, he is shocked to hear the unkind and gossipy way the other lawyers talk about their spouses and children, exposing them to shame and ridicule. Though tempted to join in, our young lawyer does not give in. Instead, he shares how his wife and unborn child are a blessing.

Though with Jesus temptation stops at suggestion, the next two stages of temptation St. Gregory writes about are unfortunately familiar to the rest of us. When a thought to sin is suggested to our mind, we have the choice to "push it out" of our mind or to consider it, to "delight" in it. This is the second stage of temptation.

Using the example of our young lawyer, if he began to take pleasure in hearing his fellow lawyers' uncharitable stories about their spouses and children, he would be entering into the realm of "delight." Maybe he even starts to wonder if he should join in to their conversations, to "get along" and be one of the group.

[1]   St. Gregory the Great, *Homilies on the Gospels*, 16.

He thinks, "What's the big deal if I share some of my wife's faults with my coworkers?" At this point, he has not acted on this thought, but he has certainly entered into "delighting" in the possibility. From there, it is a "slippery slope" to actually "consenting" to sin.

When we "consent," we make a deliberate choice of the will. In other words, when we consent to act on a sinful suggestion or impulse, that is when we take it into our self, make it our own, and actually commit a sin.

Going back to our young lawyer, his partners suggest that it is normal to speak negatively about one's spouse and children. The opportunity to unburden his issues to his colleagues is so appealing that he joins in the "fun" and exposes his family to ridicule. It is at that point that he has consented to the temptation.

Again, the temptation of Jesus in the desert by the devil and the first stage of temptation that we all experience is suggestion. But Jesus never "delighted" in the suggestions of Satan, nor did he consent to them. The goal of the spiritual life is to stop our temptations at the level of suggestion—that is, to resist them— by the grace of God. At times, the power of suggestion can seem overwhelming. But we do not need to give in! As St. Paul reminds us, "No temptation has overtaken you that is not common to man. God is faithful, and he will not let you be tempted beyond your strength, but with the temptation will also provide the way of escape, that you may be able to endure it" (1 Corinthians 10:13).

2. Satan asks Jesus, "Who is your father?"

Just as with Jesus, doesn't the devil ask us this question during difficult seasons of our lives? As he faced his passion, Jesus experienced such emotional stress and anguish in the Garden of Gethsemane that he sweat blood (see Luke 22:44)! Likewise, Satan waits till we are at our lowest point and then suggests we question our relationship with God. The devil's challenge might go something like this:

"If God is your Father, then where was he when you were betrayed? When you were rejected? When you were abandoned? If God is your Father, then why did he allow your mother to die from cancer? Why did he allow your father leave when you were a young child?" The list goes on …

When we begin to question our relationship with God, as our Father, the devil then gets us to question our own identity.

He asks, "Who are you?"

We might start to think: *Right … who am I anyway? Am I really important to God? Maybe God doesn't care about me at all. Maybe he really doesn't love me. Since I am uncertain about my relationship with God, I need to discover who I am. I need to find my identity in human relationships or in my work or interests.*

3. Satan doesn't change. He is still at work today.

The devil acts the same way today as he did with Jesus in the desert and the Garden of Gethsemane. The questions he posed to Jesus in *The Passion of the Christ* are the same questions he uses to tempt us now. He wants us to question our relationship with God, to separate us from our experience of God as our Father. Satan's purpose has always been to get us to turn away from God. This has been his plan since the beginning.

During his temptations in the desert, we read in Mark's Gospel that Jesus was with the "wild beasts" as well as Satan (Mark 1:13). (Interestingly, this is the only account that mentions any "wild beasts.") This harkens back to the Garden of Eden, where our first parents were among the wild beasts and "the serpent" (i.e., the devil):

Now the serpent was more subtle than any other wild creature that the LORD God made. He said to the woman, "Did God say, 'You shall not eat of any tree of the garden?'" And the woman said to the serpent, "We may eat of the fruit of the trees of the garden; but God said, 'You shall not eat of the fruit of the tree which is in the midst of the garden, neither shall you touch it, lest you die.'" But the serpent said to the woman, "You will not die" (Genesis 3:1-4).

Here, the serpent suggests to Eve that God is a liar. His goal is to weaken Adam and Eve's trust in God. Following this suggestion, Satan then tempts Eve to delight in the lie that she could become "like God" by disobeying his command: "For God knows that when you eat of it your eyes will be opened, and you will be like God, knowing good and evil" (Genesis 3:5).

Though Adam and Eve had already been created in the "image and likeness of God," Eve believed the lie of the devil that God was untrustworthy. "So when the woman saw that the tree was good for food, and that it was a delight to the eyes ... she took of its fruit and ate; and she also gave some to her husband, and he ate it" (Genesis 3:6).

By consenting to the temptation of the devil, Adam and Eve seriously injured their relationship with God and one another. They lost the "grace of original holiness" and became "afraid of God" (see CCC 399). The harmony that they had with the world around them was broken and, as the *Catechism* puts it, "death makes its entry into human history" (CCC 400). We are still living with the consequences of the sins of our first parents, but we have hope to overcome temptation and sin through Jesus. As St. Paul says, "For as by one man's [Adam's] disobedience many were made sinners, so by one man's [Jesus'] obedience many will be made righteous."

LIES WE ARE TEMPTED TO BELIEVE

What are some of the lies that we might be tempted to believe that can seriously damage our relationship with God and the Church?

In my walk with the Lord, I have come to see that there are three dominant deceptive suggestions from Satan that can negatively affect how we relate to God and to our brothers and sisters in the Church.

The first dominant lie is that God is an "angry scorekeeper." He is out to get us! He is waiting for us to step out of line so he can zap us! This punitive view of God is reinforced by some surprising, and seemingly innocent, traditions. For example, the popular Christmas song *Santa Claus Is Coming to Town* tells us that Santa "makes lists" that he "checks" to see who is "naughty or nice." While few people literally mistake God for Santa Claus, many have a "Santa Claus" spirituality—expecting God to give them what they want if they are good and to punish them (and everyone else) when they are bad.

In the past, some parents, in the guise of Santa, even put coal in their children's Christmas stockings if they were "naughty." This tradition reinforced the lie that Santa is out to get children if they aren't "nice" enough. If Santa is "making a list" of all of our bad deeds to determine who gets the coal, what about God? Isn't he "worse," since he created Santa? While this may seem like a bit of a stretch, myths that are lived out with real consequences and rewards are altogether logical to young children.

Perhaps surprisingly, my own belief in God as an "angry scorekeeper" who was "out to get me" did not begin in childhood. It actually developed soon after I first experienced God's profound love for me at the Steubenville conference. Though I now knew God loved me, I didn't think he liked me very much—or at least my actions. I still thought I had to measure up to "avoid getting coal in my stocking."

Shortly after I entered the seminary, I requested to be sent on a mission immersion to El Paso, Texas, and to Juárez and Sierra Tarahumara, Chihuahua, Mexico. While living in El Paso, I spent most of my time learning Spanish. Occasionally, I went to a safe house to visit Catholics who crossed the border illegally from Juárez.

In 2008, Juárez was one of the most dangerous places in the world because of the wars between the various drug cartels and gangs. Every day, members of law enforcement and innocent civilians were falling victim to the gruesome violence. (In fact, shortly after I returned home from Mexico, the immediate family of the priest who led our mission was murdered by drug cartels.) Though the news regularly featured stories about the dangers of life in Juárez, I didn't really grasp the severity of this reality until I saw it myself, in the presence of people who were fighting for their survival every day.

Eventually, I began to spend most of my time with families in Juárez. We visited the poorest of the poor, who lived in what appeared to be waste dumps. We sat at their feet, listened to their stories of despair and hope, prayed together, and celebrated the sacraments of baptism, reconciliation, and Eucharist with them. Even in the midst of their depressing conditions, the Church was present. I wish I could I say that my passion for being a missionary in Mexico was fueled solely by a desire to bring the joy of the gospel to an oppressed people. If I am honest with myself, though, my motives were not that pure.

Actually, my main reason for wanting to do mission work was to ease the wrath of God toward me. I wanted God to see that I was willing to work in a dangerous city and potentially die for him so that he would like me. I didn't yet believe that we are not required to—nor can we—"earn" God's affection. He is not repulsed by our brokenness. We do not need to "win him over." He is our loving Father.

But wait, you might ask. *Didn't God kick Adam and Eve out of the Garden of Eden after they sinned? Doesn't this prove that God doesn't want people around who disobey him?* On the contrary, like a good parent, God disciplined our first parents and protected them by commanding them to leave the Garden. He was concerned about their ultimate salvation.

As we read in Genesis, "Now, lest he [Adam] put forth his hand and take also of the tree of life, and eat, and live forever … " (Genesis 3:22). Since they sinned by eating from the Tree of the Knowledge of Good and Evil, they damaged their relationship with God. He then removed them from the Garden so they would not be tempted to eat from the Tree of Life. If Satan tempted them to eat from the Tree of Life, their ruptured relationship with God would be broken forever. Instead, God set a plan in motion to restore humanity's relationship with him.

To accomplish this plan of reconciliation, God sent his Son, Jesus Christ, to dwell among our broken humanity and redeem us through his death and resurrection. "For God did not send his Son into the world to condemn the world, but that the world might be saved through him" (John 3:16).

Our God is not an "angry scorekeeper" out to get us. That which we believe about God will affect the way we attempt to encounter him. If we believe that his ordinary disposition is that of wrath when we mess up, then there is a good chance that we will treat people with wrath when they mess up. As St. Paul tells us, "While we were yet sinners, Christ died for us" (Romans 5:8).

ANNA MARIA'S STORY

Years ago, a young wife and mother named Anna Maria Taigi decided to go to confession. She had spent many years more concerned with the things of the world than her relationship with God. She walked to her neighborhood parish church and waited in a long line of penitents. When she finally entered the confessional, she began to cry, becoming aware of all the ways she had chosen sin over Jesus in her life. The priest's initial response to her tears, inexplicably, was, "Go away. You're not one of my penitents." It is hard to imagine what Anna Maria must have felt as she heard these words. Nonetheless, she persevered, confessed her sins, and received absolution. The priest then slammed the confessional slide closed in irritation. This experience wounded her deeply, and she remained discouraged for quite a while.

Eventually, Anna Maria made her way back to the Church and began attending the parish in which she was married. Once again, she felt called to receive the sacrament of reconciliation, but her previous experience caused her to approach the confessional with some anxiety. This time, though, her confessor was a religious priest named Fr. Angelo Verandi. He gently told her, "Our Lord loves you and wants you to be wholly his." He treated her in a way that reflected the loving God he encountered every day in prayer. After this profound experience of God's love and mercy, Anna Maria became an intentional disciple of Jesus and witnessed to her family and her community the transformative love of God.

Inspired by Blessed Anna Maria's story, a priest obtained a first class relic of her and placed it on the table between his chair and the penitent's. He began to pray for those whom God would send him to receive the sacrament of reconciliation. Imagine his shock when a penitent came through the door and said, "Father, this is my first confession in a long time. The last time I went to confession, the priest chewed me out. I've not been back since. So I'm really nervous." As he heard these words, the priest looked over at his first class relic of Blessed Anna Maria Taigi. He immediately knew that she was interceding before the throne of heaven for him and this penitent. With God's grace, this person soon became an intentional disciple of Jesus and a minister in the Church.

If we believe that God is angry toward us, then we will in turn be angry and irritable with others. We can actually be an obstacle to their relationship with God. But if we believe that God is loving and merciful, then we have the capacity to build bridges for our community in their walk toward eternity.

GOD, THE ETERNAL "VENDING MACHINE"?

Another misconception that Satan sows in our minds about God is to see him as a "vending machine" for our wants. Because of our consumerist society and the great value we place on material things, our expectations of God's love and help can take on a materialistic direction, and our relationship with him can become one-sided. We will connect with him to the extent he gives us what we want. But will we continue to spend time with God after we get what we want? I don't know about you, but I have never been one to hang out around a vending machine after it dispenses my selection.

What if God doesn't give me what I want? Then what? How do we treat a vending machine if it takes our money without dispensing anything or if the candy bar we selected jams on its way out? We get annoyed, pound on it, shake it, maybe even kick it. Right? And what do we do with a particular vending machine that has failed to deliver more than once? We stop using it. Likewise, if we see God as a vending machine, as someone who must give us what we want, then our relationship with him can be weakened when he doesn't "deliver the goods." While the Lord certainly wants us to bring all of our thoughts, feelings, and desires to him in prayer, we should not limit him to what *we* think is best.

Jesus does tell his disciples, "Whatever you ask in my name, I will do it, that the Father may be glorified in the Son; if you ask anything in my name, I will do it" (John 14:13; see also Matthew 18:19; Mark 11:24). This passage, though, as all of Scripture, must be read in context, lest we have a fundamental misunderstanding of our Lord's words. If not, we might think, "Well, Jesus said that he will do whatever I ask of him. But I have asked him many times, and he still has not delivered it"—whatever "it" may be.

If we look at this passage closely, however, we notice that Jesus says he will do what we request if we ask *in his "name."* To ask in Jesus' name is to ask with a heart and mind that is united to the Father's will. In other words, what we ask for must be in line with God's loving plan for our lives, not anything from our whims.

One of the Church's greatest theologians, St. Thomas Aquinas, says that what we ask in prayer is not meant to change "the divine disposition"; rather, our requests are meant to bring about *what God wills to be achieved* only by the means of prayer.[2]

As the great third-century bishop and Doctor of the Church St. Augustine explains:

> Whatever we ask for that would hinder our salvation, we do not ask in our Savior's name and yet he is our Savior, not only when he does what we ask, but also when he does not. When he sees us ask anything to the disadvantage of our salvation, he shows himself our Savior by not doing it. The physician knows whether what the sick man asks for is to the advantage or disadvantage of his health; and does not allow what would be to his hurt, though the sick man himself desires it; but looks to his final cure.[3]

2   See St. Thomas Aquinas, *Summa Theologica*, II–II, 83, emphasis added.
3   St. Augustine, *In Joh. Ev. Tractatus*, LXXIII.

Many people are challenged by the notion that God answers each and every prayer. All of us have had the experience of praying for a particular outcome and then being disappointed that nothing seems to happen. But this is because we have mistakenly understood "answers" as giving us exactly what we prayed for, in exactly the way that we want it. Our faith teaches us that God *always* hears all of our prayers—but he answers them in one of three ways: "yes," "no," or "not now."

There is a man named Jim, who is very much involved in the Catholic charismatic renewal. Jim has witnessed many spiritual, emotional, and physical healings in his life. For many years, his relationship with God was one-sided. He sought to use God to get what he wanted. On September 11, 2001, Jim immediately went to his parish church to pray and ask God for peace of mind in the midst of such horrific events. Jim received the peace he prayed for, and he continued to pray fervently for a couple of weeks. When he was no longer concerned about his own well-being, though, he stopped attending Mass and spending time with God in prayer.

In August 2005, Hurricane Katrina devastated New Orleans. Once again, Jim ran back to church to pray that his family would be protected from harm. He also started going to Mass and was intentional with prayer for a few weeks. Comfortable that the crisis was over, he stopped spending time with God and began living in a way that was harmful not only to himself but also to others.

A few years later, through a tragic turn of events, Jim was in an automobile accident and was paralyzed. Once again, he became very intentional in his commitment to Mass and daily prayer. He became involved in the charismatic movement, which emphasized the possibility of "on-the-spot" miracles. He asked the Lord for physical healing of his paralysis, and after months of no tangible results, something changed in his prayer.

As Jim spent more time in prayer, he came to realize something very significant that has continued to shape his walk with God and his Church. He began to see that the "thorn in his side" was his paralysis, which literally kept him rooted in relationship with God and his parish community. In the past, Jim would ask God for something, then walk away from God when he got what he wanted, returning to an unhealthy lifestyle. This time, though, his condition kept him in a relationship with God, and he began to understand that it might not be the best thing for him to be healed physically. Such a healing might actually be detrimental to the spiritual renewal he was experiencing.

Providentially, God was protecting Jim from himself. The Lord said no to Jim's prayer for healing from his paralysis because God had greater things in store for him, things that transcended his ability to walk. Still a paraplegic, Jim no longer uses God to "get" things; he now abides in a deeper relationship with God as his loving Father. Ironically, his greatest source of intimacy with God is in the place he least expected it would be—his wheelchair. Jim is certainly open to a healing miracle in the future, but only if it is best for his sanctification and the sanctification of others.

In the Garden of Gethsemane, Jesus prayed: "My Father, if it be possible, let this cup pass from me; nevertheless, not as I will, but as thou wilt" (Matthew 26:39). Uttering the same prayer a second time, he prayed, "My Father, if this cannot pass unless I drink it, thy will be done" (Matthew 26:42). He then prayed a third time (see Matthew 26:44) … and then continued his journey to the Cross to fulfill the will of the Father for the salvation of the world. This scene clearly demonstrates that Jesus had human desires—and that he communicated them to God in prayer. At the same time, Jesus was not attached to his desires. He did not demand that his Father consent to his request. His will was in perfect conformity to his Father's will (see CCC 612).

Jesus clearly did not relate to his Father as a "divine vending machine," nor does he relate to his community, the Church, in this way. How we respond to God in prayer can affect the way we treat our brothers and sisters, as we can see in the following Scripture.

Following Jesus' passion, death, and resurrection, he appeared to St. Peter, the apostle he chose to be the "rock" of his Church, the apostle who had denied him three times.

St. John describes the scene:

> When they had finished breakfast, Jesus said to Simon Peter, "Simon, Son of John, do you love me more than these?" He said to him, "Yes, Lord; you know that I love you." He said to him, "Feed my lambs." A second time he said to him, "Simon, son of John, do you love me?" He said to him, "Yes, Lord; you know that I love you." He said to him, "Tend my sheep." He said to him the third time, "Simon, son of John, do you love me?" Peter was grieved because he said to him the third time, "Do you love me?" And he said to him, "Lord, you know everything; you know that I love you." Jesus said to him, "Feed my sheep" (John 21:15-17).

Because Peter denied Jesus three times, Jesus asks him three times if he loves him. A threefold declaration of love to "cancel" out the threefold denial. What is particularly interesting about this passage are the different words for "love" used in the original Greek text. Jesus first asks Peter if he loves him using the word *agape,* which means a sacrificial, unconditional love— the way God loves us and the way we are called to love others. Tellingly, Peter responds using the word *philia,* which refers to a "friendship" love.

Two times Jesus asks Peter if he loves him with an unconditional love, and both times Peter responds that he loves Jesus as a "friend." But the third time, Jesus uses *philia*, which upsets Peter—because he realizes that he doesn't yet love Jesus with an unconditional, sacrificial *agape* love.

We can see here a parallel between Jesus' questioning of Peter and his prayer to the Father in the Garden. Once again, Jesus has no expectation that his desires will be fulfilled. If Peter was only able to love him with *philia* (not *agape*), then Jesus was willing to meet him where he was and receive his gift with gratitude.

As followers of Jesus, the same applies to us in our relationship with God and others. We should express our desires but not hold on to our expectations. When we can be in a relationship with God even when we don't get what we want or expect, then we open ourselves up to being in communion with others who will often fail to live up to our expectations or desires.

THE PROSPERITY GOSPEL LIE

A commonly accepted view in certain Christian circles is the belief that accepting Jesus as Lord inevitably brings with it the blessings of good health, financial wealth, and peace-filled relationships. Some have labeled this the "prosperity gospel." This is an extremely harmful view of the Christian faith because it implies that if one is not healthy, wealthy, and blessed with peaceful relationships, then he or she is somehow lacking in faith.

The devil will work overtime to get us to question God's love for us—and for us to question our relationship with God. The belief that God wants us to prosper materially in this life cannot account for the millions of faithful Christians who live in dire poverty with barely any food or running water, nor the millions of believers who die every year from cancer, nor the millions of Christians who are persecuted and killed for their faith. The notion that such

Christians are simply lacking in faith simply cannot be "squared" with the plain truth of the gospel.

When we subscribe to the false notion that God wants us to be overly concerned with our health, wealth, and relationships, we miss out on the opportunity to be present to those in our community who are suffering and need our support. Perhaps it is not surprising that in our prosperous, consumeristic society, Satan seeks to tempt us with the notion that ease and comfort are a sign of God's favor.

A number of years ago, I received a phone call from a woman in her early forties named Tasha. She was going through a season of profound suffering and loss. A coworker was a parishioner at my parish, and she encouraged the woman to reach out to me for pastoral counseling. After a quick prayer, I invited Tasha to share her story. She said, "Father, I don't know where to begin. My son is in prison on drug charges, and my husband recently passed away. On my way home from his funeral, I was involved in an accident that totaled my car. I'm a good person. I don't know why all these bad things keep happening to me."

I asked her about how her prayer life was holding up in the midst of all this desolation. She said, "I don't know what to say, Father. I've been a woman of prayer my whole life, but I don't even know if I can believe in God anymore. If God cared about me, then I wouldn't be suffering so much."

As I listened to her difficult story, I prayed, asking for the Holy Spirit to help me communicate only what God wanted me to express to this hurting woman. I also prayed that Tasha could receive only that which God wanted her to hear. The lives of Jesus, Mary, and St. Paul came into my mind and heart. I asked if could share a few passages from the Bible with her, and she agreed.

"Have you ever heard the story of St. Paul?" I asked. She was silent. I continued, "St. Paul became an apostle of Jesus after his ascension. The Lord appeared to him while he was persecuting Christians. After his encounter with Jesus, Paul decided to spend the rest of his life proclaiming the gospel for the salvation of souls. But check this out—though he was a devoted believer and an intentional disciple of Jesus, his life was still filled with extraordinary sufferings."

I told her, "In his second letter to the Corinthians, St. Paul reveals to them that after he became an apostle, he was imprisoned multiple times, endured beatings, received forty lashes on five different occasions, was beaten with rods three times, and was stoned. His life was not filled with financial wealth and physical health. For that matter, nor were those of the other apostles, ten of whom were tortured and killed because of their relationship with Christ. So I don't think it is God's will that we experience temporal prosperity as a fruit of our relationship with him." Tasha listened intently but remained silent.

I continued, "If the lives of St. Paul and the apostles don't speak to your heart, then maybe you can relate to the Blessed Virgin Mary, who spent her entire life doing God's will. A few years after her husband Joseph died, she witnessed her innocent son, Jesus, receive an unjust sentence. Her son was not only imprisoned, he was betrayed, rejected, denied, and abandoned by his closest friends. Can you imagine how Mary felt?"

"She then accompanied her Son as he was verbally mocked, physically assaulted, stripped naked, tortured, and crucified on a cross. Do you think Mary wasn't blessed by God? Do you think she gave up on her relationship with God because of the profound suffering she experienced? No, she didn't. She trusted in God and remained devoted to him. The bottom line is this: Jesus never told us this life would be easy. In fact, the one point he made very clear was that being his disciple would involve taking up our cross every day in our walk toward eternity."

I then paused so that Tasha and I could sit in silence and reflect. After about a minute of silence, Tasha said, "Wow, I never thought of it that way. My relationship with God was never explained to me like that. I guess I never really thought about the suffering of Mary and the apostles." After sharing our hearts for a little while, I asked Tasha if she would allow me and some other parishioners to walk with her during this "season of the cross" in her life. She gratefully accepted.

Interestingly, Tasha was born and raised as a Christian. She lived in a God-fearing community. But the lies she learned and ultimately came to believe about God crippled her from really getting to know him. She never saw God as he has revealed himself in the Scriptures and the Church.

THE FACE … AND CROSS … OF CHRIST

Unfortunately, Tasha's experience of growing up in the Church and yet not knowing much about God is not unique. It is all too common these days—and even throughout salvation history. In the Old Testament, a priest named Eli raised the prophet Samuel right in the Temple, which contained the Ark of the Covenant. Though Samuel literally grew up in the Temple, he did not "know the Lord" and could not hear his voice at first (see 1 Samuel 3).

So how can we come to know truly the God who created us from love to love? By focusing our attention on the words and actions of Jesus.

Jesus is the face of God. In his encyclical letter *Novo Millennio Ineunte,* St. John Paul II mentions the "face of Christ" thirty-seven times. He writes:

The contemplation of Christ's face cannot fail to be inspired by all that we are told about him in Sacred Scripture, which from beginning to end is permeated by his mystery, prefigured in a veiled way in the Old Testament and revealed fully in the New, so that Saint Jerome can vigorously affirm: "Ignorance of the Scriptures is ignorance of Christ."[4]

Like others, I have come to know people after I spend time with them and witness how they act. So how can we come to know Jesus through his actions? We can accomplish this by intentionally and consistently becoming students in the "school" of the Cross. When we spend a few minutes every day pondering Jesus crucified, we will deepen our understanding of—and our relationship with—our God.

After Jesus Christ was betrayed, denied, and abandoned by his closest friends, the apostles, he was imprisoned and put on trial before Pontius Pilate. The outcome of this trial was to have him tortured, mocked, and crucified. Jesus was crucified between two thieves who both initially reviled him (see Matthew 27:44). Though he was being insulted by the thieves and physically assaulted by the Roman soldiers, Jesus responded to their hatred by praying for them: "Father, forgive them; for they know not what they do" (John 23:34). The prayer of Jesus for his persecutors in the midst of suffering had a powerful impact on one of the criminals who was being crucified next to Jesus.

As the Gospel of Luke relates:

One of the criminals who were hanged railed at him, saying, "Are you not the Christ? Save yourself and us!" But the other rebuked him, saying, "Do you not fear God, since you are under the same sentence of condemnation? And we indeed have been condemned justly; for we are receiving the due reward of our deeds; but this man has done nothing wrong."

---

[4] St. John Paul II, Apostolic Letter *Novo Millennio Ineunte* (2001), 17.

And he said, "Jesus, remember me when you come in your kingly power." And he said to him, "Truly, I say to you, today you will be with me in Paradise" (Luke 23:39-43).

Notice what Jesus does here. He does not hold a grudge against the good thief, saying that he needs to work to earn his forgiveness. Jesus freely gives it to him. Since Jesus is the same yesterday, today, and forever, he offers us his forgiveness as well. All we need to do is imitate the good thief and seek Jesus' mercy in the sacrament of reconciliation.

The cross of Christ teaches us much about God's mercy, and it reveals the Lord's attentiveness to our needs. On the Cross, he was completely focused on the needs of those around him— and he is completely focused on our needs as well. Jesus always provides for us what we need in our faith journey.

At the foot of the Cross stands the Mother of Jesus. She had nurtured him in her womb, nursed him at her breast, and carried him in her arms as they traveled from Bethlehem to Egypt to Nazareth. She had listened to him teach in the Temple at the age of twelve, witnessed his first miracle at the wedding feast of Cana, and now was preparing her pierced heart to witness his death for the salvation of souls.

Upon seeing his Mother, Jesus turns his attention to her needs. Since Jesus was the only child of a widow, he was responsible for finding someone to take care of her. Jesus said to Mary, "Woman, behold your son!" (John 19:26). With these words, Jesus entrusts his mother to John, the Beloved Disciple, who stands with her at the foot of the Cross. Speaking to John—and to all of us—he then says, "Behold, your mother!" (John 19:27). John then welcomes Mary into his home to provide for her needs.

In his crucifixion, Jesus reveals to humanity God's patience to those who speak and act against his will, a God who forgives those who seek forgiveness for their offenses. He shows us a God who attends to the sufferings of those who reach out to him. Rather than believing in the lies the Enemy whispers in our ears about God, let us trust in the God of the Gospels, who is ever-patient, forgiving, and compassionate.

Invitation to
PRAYER

A person who spent a lot of time with Jesus Christ crucified was St. Teresa of Calcutta. She spent hours every day gazing at the statue of a crucified Savior. She composed the following reflection in response to Jesus' question in Matthew 16:15: "Who do you say that I am?"

You are God.
You are God from God.
You are Begotten, not made.
You are One in Substance with the Father.
You are the Son of the Living God.
You are the Second Person of the Blessed Trinity.
You are One with the Father.

You are in the Father from the beginning:
All things were made by you and the Father.
You are the Beloved Son in whom the Father is well pleased.
You are the Son of Mary, conceived by the Holy Spirit in the
*   womb of Mary.*
You were born in Bethlehem.
You were wrapped in swaddling clothes by Mary and put in the
*   manger full of straw.*
You were kept warm by the breath of the donkey that carried
*   your mother with you in her womb.*
You are the Son of Joseph, the carpenter, as known by the
*   people of Nazareth.*
You are an ordinary man without much learning, as judged by
*   the learned people of Israel.*

Who Is Jesus to Me?

Jesus is the Word made Flesh.

Jesus is the Bread of Life.

Jesus is the Victim offered for our sins on the Cross.

Jesus is the Sacrifice offered at the Holy Mass for the sins of the world and mine.

Jesus is the Word ... to be spoken.

Jesus is the Truth ... to be told.

Jesus is the Way ... to be walked.

Jesus is the Light ... to be lit.

Jesus is the Life ... to be lived.

Jesus is the Love ... to be loved.

Jesus is the Joy ... to be shared.

Jesus is the Sacrifice ... to be offered.

Jesus is the Peace ... to be given.

Jesus is the Bread of Life ... to be eaten.

Jesus is the Hungry ... to be fed.

Jesus is the Thirst ... to be satiated.

Jesus is the Naked ... to be clothed.

Jesus is the Homeless ... to be taken in.

Jesus is the Sick ... to be healed.

Jesus is the Lonely ... to be loved.

Jesus is the Unwanted ... to be wanted.

Jesus is the Leper ... to wash his wounds.

Jesus is the Beggar ... to give him a smile.

Jesus is the Drunkard ... to listen to him.

Jesus is the Mentally Disabled ... to protect him.

Jesus is the Little One ... to embrace him.

Jesus is the Blind ... to lead him.

Jesus is the Dumb ... to speak for him.

Jesus is the Crippled ... to walk with him.

Jesus is the Drug Addict ... to befriend him.

Jesus is the Prostitute ... to remove from danger and befriend.

Jesus is the Prisoner ... to be visited.
Jesus is the Old ... to be served.
Jesus is my God.
Jesus is my Spouse.
Jesus is my Life.
Jesus is my only Love.
Jesus is my All in All.
Jesus is my Everything.

Jesus, I love with my whole heart, with my whole being. I have given him all, even my sins, and he has espoused me to himself in tenderness and love. Now and for life I am the spouse of my Crucified Spouse. Amen.

To cultivate a deeper knowledge of God, I invite you to look at a crucifix for ten minutes every day. You don't need to pray with a lot of words. Just take some time to focus on how much Jesus loves you.

QUESTIONS
For Meditation and Discussion

1. Have you seen the film *The Passion of the Christ*? If so, do you remember the opening scene between Jesus and Satan? What struck you most about this scene?

2. Have you experienced a low point in your life when you faced temptation? How did this affect your relationship with God?

3. Have you ever asked, "Who am I?" Do you find it more comfortable to identify yourself by your accomplishments (in work, family, activities, etc.) than by your relationship with God?

4. Have you felt the emptiness caused by sin? How do you remain confident about making good choices?

5. Can you relate to St. Gregory the Great's stages of temptation?

6. Does the story of the lawyer parallel any of your experiences? If so, how?

7. What are some of the lies that we might be tempted to believe about God that have the capacity to seriously damage our relationships with him and others?

8. Have you ever felt like you had to earn God's love? How
    have you found yourself acting on this belief?

9. What is your reaction to the assertion that God answers
    every prayer?

10. What are some of the dangers of seeing God as an "angry
    scorekeeper"? How could this perception influence how
    we treat others?

11. Has your experience with the sacrament of reconciliation
    been life-giving? Why, or why not?

Chapter Four

Intimacy with God

Growing up in the 1990s, I had the biggest crush on Mariah Carey, a biracial singer who dominated the music charts during my childhood. She had the voice of an angel, and I found her physical appearance to be stunningly beautiful. She was my first crush. I imagined that she and I would meet one day, fall in love at first sight, get married, and have many children together.

As seasons change and we get older, though, so do our adolescent crushes. When I entered the "big league" of high school, a new woman came into my life. Like Mariah, I imagined that we could potentially meet, date, and marry. This new woman I daydreamed about was not only a chart-topping singer, she was also a dancer, model, and an award-winning actress. Her name: Jennifer Lopez. Similar to my earlier crush on Mariah, my affection for Jennifer lasted for quite a few years.

Eventually, I graduated, went to college, and then entered the seminary. Everything was going well with my priestly formation until I heard the most terrible news, news that rocked my world: My childhood crush, Mariah Carey, had beef with my teenage crush, Jennifer Lopez. As I attempted to remain faithful to my seminary studies, prayer, and my relationship with Jesus, imagine my stress upon hearing that they had issues with one other! This was a difficult season for me.

Of course, I am joking—for the most part. But the media really did build up a false narrative about a disagreement that Mariah Carey had with Jennifer Lopez. In the midst of all the media hype, though, Mariah shared an insight that has radically impacted by priestly ministry.

So what's the story? Where did this fake news story originate? Apparently, Mariah Carey did a red carpet interview at some award ceremony many years ago. A German reporter asked her what she thought about Jennifer Lopez, and she infamously replied, "I don't know her."

Those four words became the source of a media-hyped "feud" that lasted for well over a decade. How could Mariah Carey not know Jennifer Lopez? At the time of this particular interview in the early 2000s, Jennifer Lopez was one of the most famous celebrities in the world. Her songs regularly topped the Billboard charts, and she had leading roles in several films that were box office hits. To top it off, Jennifer had worked with Mariah Carey's ex-husband, producer and record executive Tommy Mottola, and the two attended the same award shows for years.

As the years went on, this issue would be presented to Jennifer repeatedly, and she could not understand why Mariah would claim not to know her when they had met many times. Finally, on a late-night show, Mariah was asked to set the record straight. She said, "That was so long ago. I can't believe people still make a big deal out of it." But the host persisted, "So, do you know each other?" She shouted, "No!" He responded, "But she says you do!" Mariah then responded with one of the most profound statements I have ever heard from a celebrity: "If I never had a conversation with you and someone asked me about you, I would say, 'I don't know him. He seems cool, but I don't know him.'"

Mariah went on to explain that the German reporter first asked her about Beyoncé, who was a friend of hers. She was able to speak at length about Beyoncé because she had a personal relationship with her. The reporter then asked about Jennifer Lopez, and she gave the infamous, "I don't know her," reply. Mariah went on to explain: "Of course I know who she is, but I don't *know* her." The reporter then asked, "Do you know me?" She said, "Yes. We've met. We've talked. We've had cool moments together."

Mariah Carey's profound insight is simple: Just because we know *about* someone does not mean we *know* the person. To truly know someone, we need to encounter him or her and have conversations with the person. We have to share "moments" or memories with the person.

Did Mariah Carey know *about* Jennifer Lopez? Sure. Did she know that Jennifer was a model, dancer, singer, and actress who worked with her ex-husband? Of course. Did she attend the same award shows and perform on the same stages as her? Yes. Did she ever wave at Jennifer Lopez at red carpet events? Yes. So she knew *about* her, but she did not *know* her.

KNOWING *ABOUT* GOD VERSUS KNOWING GOD

As a priest who travels the country speaking at conferences, many people know about me. They may have watched my videos or read articles about me. They may have even followed my ministry on social media. However, just because they know about me does not mean that they know me. As we have seen, to know someone means we have a personal relationship with him or her.

Mariah Carey's insight into knowing another is important in our spiritual journey. Nearly everyone has heard about God. If we were raised in a Catholic home, we probably read books about God and studied the stories of the Old and New Testaments in religious education class. We might even be able to recite the Ten Commandments and the Beatitudes. However, just because we may know a lot *about* God doesn't mean we actually *know* God.

Don't get me wrong. Knowing about God is essential in our walk toward eternal life, but it is not sufficient. As Jesus tells us, "Not every one who says to me, 'Lord, Lord,' shall enter the kingdom of heaven … On that day many will say to me, 'Lord, Lord, did we not prophesy in your name, and cast out demons in your name, and do many mighty works in your name?' And then will I declare to them, 'I never knew you'" (Matthew 7:21-23).

Jesus makes it clear to his disciples that knowledge of God's laws and doing good works in the name of God are not the same as having a *relationship* with him. I can't tell you how many people, good people, I have met over the years who have taught religious education classes and served at homeless shelters and soup kitchens but have never spent time—intentional time—cultivating a personal, one-on-one relationship with God.

St. Teresa of Calcutta also noticed this reality in some of her Missionaries of Charity sisters. She addressed her community on this subject: "I worry some of you still have not really met Jesus—one to one—you and Jesus alone. We may spend time in chapel, but have you seen with the eyes of your soul how he looks at you with love? Do you really know the living Jesus, not just from books but from being with him in your heart? Have you heard the loving words he speaks to you? Ask for the grace; he is longing to give it."

When I was in the seminary, I was able to spend some time working with Mother Teresa's nuns in Calcutta. The sheer amount of work that these dedicated sisters do for the poorest of the poor is incredible! But what surprised me the most was the amount of time they spent in prayer. Each day started with

Mass and recitation of the Rosary at six o'clock in the morning and ended with an hour of silence before the Blessed Sacrament at six o'clock in the evening. Throughout the day, the sisters would break to have community prayer, and during their hours of serving the poor, they would talk to God as they washed clothes, prepared meals, fed the hungry, and held the hands of the dying and destitute.

Since I was a seminarian, the sisters would set aside some time to share their wisdom with me. One of the sisters revealed to me why they were so intentional and consistent with the time they spent in prayer—it was their source of intimacy with Jesus. Their personal relationship with Jesus motivated them and gave them the strength to express their love through acts of service to the poorest of the poor. If they didn't know Jesus personally through their daily encounters, they would not be able to do the work that was in front of them joyfully.

How, then, do we get to know God in a personal way? The answer, as witnessed by Mother Teresa's nuns, is through prayer. But what is prayer? The *Catechism of the Catholic Church* defines prayer as a "living and vital relationship" with God (CCC 2558). How do we cultivate this living and vital relationship with God? The same way we foster a living and vital relationship with people—through listening and speaking.

How do we begin to listen to the voice of God in prayer? One of the ways that we can open ourselves up to hearing God's voice is through reading the Bible. How many of us have a copy of the Bible at home collecting dust on a shelf? Imagine if the pope or the president of the United States wrote us a personal letter, and after glancing at it a few times, we put it in our drawer and never looked at it again. We probably would not do that! No, we would tell all our friends about the letter. We would take a picture of it and put it on social media. We would frame it and place it in the most prominent place in our home so all who come by can see it. We would look at it and read it often.

We have received a much greater "letter," from a much more important author than the pope or the president. We have received a letter that was written for everyone (including you!), not just to monks and priests and religious. This letter was sent from God himself. The bottom line: The only way to get to know Jesus Christ as he has revealed himself to us is through time spent reading God's letter to us—the Bible.

PRAYING THE BIBLE: *LECTIO DIVINA*

So the next question is, "How do I read and pray with the Bible so that I can get to know Jesus and better open myself up to hearing his voice?" The Church in her wisdom has given us a treasure of resources to grow in our relationship with Jesus through the Scriptures. One of the greatest of these treasures is the practice of *lectio divina,* or "divine reading" (CCC 2708). In the twelfth century, the Carthusian monk Guigo II wrote a letter to another monk on how to practice "divine reading." He entitled his work "The Ladder from Earth to Heaven: The Work on Praying the Scriptures," based on the vision of Jacob's ladder in Genesis 28:10-17.[1]

Guigo II teaches that there are four steps to *lectio divina:* reading, meditation, prayer, and contemplation. I like to add a fifth step, which is performing a concrete action based on my reading, meditating, praying, and contemplating a particular passage of Scripture.

---

[1]   Letter and Spirit 2:176.

Here is an overview of *lectio divina:*

1. **Read:** What does the particular biblical text say in and of itself?

2. **Meditate:** What does this passage "say" to you?

3. **Pray:** Converse with the Holy Spirit about what you have meditated upon.

4. **Contemplate:** Allow yourself to experience the gaze of Jesus as you look at him.

5. **Act:** What concrete action can you take in your daily life in response to what you have read, meditated, prayed, and contemplated.

The following is an example of a personal *lectio divina* reflection.

Read

The Baptism of Jesus

> Then Jesus came from Galilee to the Jordan to John, to be baptized by him. John would have prevented him, saying, "I need to be baptized by you, and do you come to me?" But Jesus answered him, "Let it be so now; for thus it is fitting for us to fulfill all righteousness." Then he consented. And when Jesus was baptized, he went up immediately from the water, and behold, the heavens were opened and he saw the Spirit of God descending like a dove, and alighting on him; and lo, a voice from heaven, saying, "This is my beloved Son, with whom I am well pleased" (Matthew 3:13-17).

Meditate

What does this passage about Jesus' baptism say to me?

As I reflect on this passage, what most strikes me is how John the Baptist did not immediately consent to Jesus' request to be baptized. As soon as he surrendered to God's will and did exactly as Jesus requested, John and everyone present experienced something truly supernatural: The heavens opened, the Spirit descended upon Jesus, and the Father spoke words of affirmation about his Beloved Son.

This passage reminds me that when I do things my way, they typically do not bear much fruit. On the other hand, I can vividly recall a number of occasions when I experienced much positive fruit after consulting the Lord in prayer and surrendering to his will in my actions.

A particular experience that comes to mind is when I attended a conference many years ago on the Word of God in New Orleans. This was early in my priestly formation. At the end of the conference, I drove back to Notre Dame Seminary to hang out with some of my classmates. As the evening went on, more young adults from the New Orleans area who were also at the conference stopped by the seminary. We shared ideas about how we could collaborate together to implement some of the practical insights from the Word of God we heard from the speakers. We sought ways to bring these practices into our everyday lives as seminarians, as single persons, and as engaged and married couples.

Our conversation that evening started with an intellectual sharing of practical ways to apply what we learned at the conference. As we spent more time together, though, we began to transition from the head to the heart. A young man named Benjamin shared with the group that he had been married for a couple of years. Shortly after the wedding, he had a sudden realization that turned his life upside down: Marriage was not for him.

Benjamin and his wife, Sarah, met when they were college. After dating for several years, they fell in love and decided to get married shortly after graduating. A few months into their new life together, Sarah suddenly became very sick and had to be hospitalized. Her illness was physically debilitating. The couple's relationship drastically changed. Instead of coming home from work to dinner on the table, he now came home from work to cook for Sarah, feed her, help her bathe, clip her nails, and get her dressed for bed. When Ben would lie in bed at night, he would think to himself, *This is not how I imagined my marriage would turn out.*

It was during these nights of pondering that Benjamin realized that his marriage was not *for him.* Sarah's suffering helped Ben to understand the truth: He married Sarah not for his personal satisfaction but for her good. The sacrament they had celebrated was not about him. His life was not about him. He had been called to marry Sarah so that he could die to himself so that she could have life.

One of the things that Benjamin said that night to the group that has stuck with me ever since were these words: "On our wedding day, I vowed to love Sarah in sickness and in health. I love her, and I will not take a vacation from my vocation." As Benjamin spoke these words, tears began to fall down his face. Everyone looked at him in silence. Words could not adequately express the emotions I felt at that moment. Our conversation had turned from practical insights about showing biblical love to an encounter with a someone who actually loved his spouse the way that Jesus loved the Church on the Cross.

I excused myself from the conversation and walked immediately to Immaculate Conception Chapel. I walked down the aisle in the dimly lit chapel and stood two feet from the tabernacle containing the Eucharistic presence of Christ. I knelt and then fell face down on the floor and lay prostrate before the Blessed Sacrament. I cried out to Jesus from the depths of my soul, asking, "Jesus, could I ever love you like that? Could I ever love you the way Benjamin loves Sarah?" As is usual with God, when we speak, he usually responds with a fairly long period of silence that can seem like an eternity. It is in that silence that we hear his voice.

After lying prostrate on the floor for about twenty minutes, I perceived God speaking to me. Not audibly, of course, but in the depths of my heart. I perceived our Lord asking me a similar question: "Josh, will you let me love you like that? Will you be vulnerable with me the way Sarah is vulnerable with Benjamin? Will you be exposed to me the way Sarah is exposed before Benjamin? Will you let me love you?" I was taken aback by these questions. Interiorly, I pondered. *Can I be vulnerable and exposed before God like Sarah has been with Benjamin?* My old fears of rejection began to flood my mind again. I thought, *There's no way I can be totally exposed before God. If God saw all of me, he wouldn't want me to be a priest. I am way too broken.* I got off of the floor and stood facing Jesus in the tabernacle. With a heavy heart, I told him, "No, I will not let you love me the way Benjamin loves Sarah." I genuflected and left the chapel with tears falling down my cheeks.

Like St. John the Baptist, I was resistant to Jesus' invitation. But why was I so hesitant to let God love me? On June 26, 2004, he had clearly revealed his love to me at the Steubenville youth conference when I had my powerful conversion experience during Adoration. Intellectually, I knew about the mercy of God from my seminary training. Unfortunately, simply recalling the love that God had for the people in the Bible and remembering the love he showed me at the youth conference was not enough. I need to daily encounter his love at the very core of my soul or I can begin to imitate the Israelites in the Old Testament and forget God's goodness.

I struggled with being vulnerable and open to God because I focused on my ongoing battle with sin rather than on his love. I spent more time brooding on my brokenness than on gazing at the loving face of my Savior. While my sins were real and needed to be addressed, it was not healthy to brood for hours on how "messed up" I was. And this goes for all of us, as fallen human beings.

Recently, one of my fellow presenters at a youth conference shared a powerful analogy with the young people who were in attendance. He said, "Listen, I know all of you have come here with a lot of very real problems that weigh heavy on your hearts and minds. For the next three days, though, I want to invite you not to focus all of your attention on your very real issues. You know what else is real? The sun. What happens if we look directly at the sun for too long? Our vision becomes affected, and we can permanently damage our eyes. Likewise, if we focus all of our attention on our failings and problems most of the time, we will experience a lot of unnecessary pain and limit our capacity to see the loving face of our Father."

The Lord was not inviting me to dwell on my faults and failures. He was simply asking me if I would allow him to love me. After I refused Jesus' invitation, he continued to pursue me. Literally, every day that followed my "no" to God, I continued to hear his question in my heart—"Will you let me love you?" He did not give up on me.

He did not give up on St. Peter, either. As the Gospels reveal, Peter's first encounter with Jesus was a result of his brother Andrew's invitation. Before he became a follower of Jesus, Andrew was a disciple of St. John the Baptist. John's mission was to prepare his disciples for the coming of the Messiah, to be a "bridge" for his followers to enter into a relationship with Christ. Once Jesus arrived on the scene, John the Baptist proclaimed, "Behold, the Lamb of God" (John 1:29). Upon hearing these words, Andrew began to follow Jesus. After some time, he introduced his brother Peter to the Lord. This is when Peter's walk with Jesus began.

Though the Bible does not explicitly say what happened, at some point, Peter stopped following Jesus and went back to being a fisherman. Jesus, however, came to him while he was fishing and invited him to become a "fisher of men" (Matthew 4:19). Peter then began to accompany Jesus as an apostle, right up to the Garden of Gethsemane, when he again left him (along with the other apostles). Just as before, Jesus went after Peter, offered him the opportunity to repent, and invited him to continue to walk as a disciple toward eternity.

Similar to Peter's turning back to the love of Jesus, I eventually gave him permission to enter the depths of my heart. During this season of my life, Jesus' words in the book of Revelation had a special meaning for me: "Behold, I stand at the door and knock" (Revelation 3:20). I was drawn to this verse because I kept hearing Jesus' question to me, "*Will* you let me?" It was an invitation, not a command. In prayer, it became clear to me that Jesus was not going to force his love on me. He was not going to impose himself into areas of my heart where I was not ready to allow him to enter. The image of Jesus knocking on the door fit well with what I was experiencing in prayer.

A wise priest once said, "We ought to pray with our imagination because if we do not *pray* with it, the devil will certainly *play* with it!" As I knelt down in the chapel before the Blessed Sacrament, an image kept coming to my mind that was rooted in the passage from Revelation about Jesus standing at the door and knocking. I imagined myself sitting in the living room of my house. Someone came to the door and gently knocked. When I opened the door, Jesus himself was standing there, and he asked, "May I come in?" At first, I declined his request, but I eventually allowed him to enter my home, saying, "Sure, Jesus, come on in."

As Jesus walked around my house, I was nervous about him seeing the messy rooms, so I invited him only into those I was proud of. First, I showed him the rooms that were dedicated to prayer. "Look, Jesus," I said. "Here is where I have recited all my prayers over the years. I've prayed many Rosaries, novenas, Divine Mercy chaplets, and the Psalms!" He looked at me with tenderness and said, "I love you, Josh." Then I showed him the rooms dedicated to the good works I performed in his name over the years—feeding the poor in Calcutta, clothing the naked in Jamaica, welcoming the strangers in El Paso, and visiting prisoners. Once again, Jesus looked at me with tenderness and said, "I love you, Josh."

Looking down the hallway, Jesus asked me, "What about those rooms further down? May we go in them, too?" I said, "Jesus, you don't want to go in them. They're very messy." Again, he asked, "May we go there?" I again protested, "Lord, you really don't want to see them. They are a mess!" The rooms down the hall were filled with all of the sins I had committed against God and others, as well as all the sins others had committed against me. These rooms were filled with shame, pain, hurts, and wounds. I did not want Jesus to go in them because I feared that he would no longer love me if he saw them. Though these sins had been washed away by the sacrament of reconciliation, I was embarrassed and ashamed of what was in these rooms. I wanted so badly for him not to "go there" with me.

The woman at the well also resisted Jesus going "there" during her conversation with him about her sins. When Jesus was traveling through Samaria, he took a moment to rest at the well of Jacob, the place where the Old Testament patriarch Jacob met his wife Rachel. Around noon, a Samaritan woman came to draw water from the well. This was an unusual time for a person to visit Jacob's well. Ordinarily, people from the village would go there when it was less sunny, in early morning or in the evening. But if a person were trying to avoid the crowds, he or she would draw water during the uncomfortable heat of midday.

As the woman approached the well, Jesus asked her for a drink. She initially resisted because he was a Jewish man and she was a Samaritan woman. Due to a shared hostility rooted in history, Samaritans and Jews usually would have nothing to do with each other. Nonetheless, Jesus began to speak with her, telling the woman about a "living water" which would quench her thirst forever. The woman then asked Jesus to share this water with her. This is where their exchange began to get a little bit uncomfortable for her. Jesus said, "Go, call your husband, and come here." The woman told Jesus, "I have no husband." Then Jesus went "there" with her. He said, "You are right in saying, 'I have no husband;' for you have had five husbands, and he whom you now have is not your husband, this you said truly." Everything Jesus told the woman about her life was true, but she still did not want to go "there" with him. Attempting to change the topic of conversation, she said, "Sir, I perceive that you are a prophet. Our fathers worshiped on this mountain; and you say that Jerusalem is the place where men ought to worship." By asking Jesus this question about worship she changed the course of their dialogue from being about her to being about God. This is a tactic many of us use when we feel uncomfortable with being too vulnerable with others (see John 4:1-20).

Years ago, when I was still in the seminary, I accompanied a priest friend of mine to visit an elderly couple, Mr. Jimmy and Mrs. Monica. Jimmy and Monica were in their late seventies, and Jimmy was dying from cancer. Mrs. Monica was a faithful Catholic who attended daily Mass and participated faithfully in the sacramental life of the Church. Jimmy, however, had not practiced his faith in many years.

I soon began visiting them on a weekly basis. During these visits, we would talk about everything and anything—about the weather, sports, the school system, and politics. At some point, Mrs. Monica would always leave the room so Mr. Jimmy and I could have some alone time. It was during these reverent moments that we would begin to talk about his impending death. Often, he would bring up regrets from his past, but he never went into too much detail. Personally, I have never been a fan of people exposing their sins to the world, so I didn't pry. But I would use these moments to encourage Mr. Jimmy to bring his sins to the sacrament of reconciliation. However, whenever I encouraged him to visit our pastor for confession, he would change the subject and ask me questions about theology.

Similar to the woman at the well and Mr. Jimmy, I wanted to avoid letting Jesus into the rooms of my heart that stored my sins, shames, hurts, pains, and wounds. I focused our time together on everything but my brokenness. But Jesus, persistent as always, asked me for the third time in my imaginative prayer experience, "May I go in?" After resisting him for so long, I ultimately chose to imitate John the Baptist and surrender to Jesus' request.

Finally, I opened the doors to the rooms in my heart that I abhorred and had kept locked up for so long. As we walked through these messy rooms together, I noticed that they had a stifling atmosphere. Though I felt Jesus' presence close behind me, I was not eager to look at his face. I kept my face downward and looked at the floor. I did not want to see his expression change from pride in me to disappointment. After gazing at the floor for a while, I decided it was time to face the music and hear Jesus say the words I was dreading: "Josh, I do not love you anymore." However, as I raised my eyes to look at Jesus, I saw something that caught me totally off guard. Despite seeing my rooms of shame and guilt, rooms that contained all the times I had turned away from God, his face had not changed. Then I again heard the words that have sustained me ever since, "Josh, I love you."

Wait!

What!?

Whoa!

In the midst of my brokenness, sins, imperfections, mistakes, failures, shame, pain, hurts, and wounds, Jesus STILL loves me!

What does this even mean? If Jesus says to me, "I love you," then I am pretty sure it is important that I understand what he means by these words. We use the word "love" casually in our culture for all different kinds of things. We say, "I love video games. I love going to the movies. I love listening to music. I love cake. I love my pets. I love my friends. I love my mom and dad. I love my spouse. I love God." Obviously, though, we don't "love" all of these things in the same way. There is no way that the way I love cake is the way I love my spouse, much less God. So how should we define this word "love" in a way that helps us understand God's love for us as described in the Scriptures and as we experience it in prayer.

The world often has a view of love that involves doing whatever we want, whenever we want, with whomever we want—as long as it feels good. From the perspective of faith, though, the weaknesses of this view of love are fairly obvious. Just because something *feels* good does not make it, in fact, "good" for us; sometimes, what feels bad in the moment is actually what is best for us. For example, it certainly does not feel good for a young mother who has a full-time job to wake up at two o'clock in the morning to attend to her crying baby. It would certainly feel better for her to sleep. But love for her baby makes it necessary for her to sacrifice some sleep. Clearly, then, love does not always feel good.

So, what is love, then? What does true love look like? In his classic work *Summa Theologica,* St. Thomas Aquinas defines love as "willing the good of the other."[2] In the case of the working mother whose baby is crying in the middle of the night, her choice to forgo sleep to take care of her baby is willing the good of her child; it is her way of showing love.

But what about God? In my experience of prayer, I have perceived that God loves me. If God says he loves me, and love is willing the good of the other, then what is the good that God wills for me? According to the Scriptures, the good that God wills for me is my salvation. In his first letter to Timothy, St. Paul writes that God wants all men to be saved (see 1 Timothy 2:4). So when Jesus says that he loves me, in essence he is saying that he desires that he wants me to be saved and abide in heaven with him forever. Not only does Jesus want *me* to be with him forever in heaven, he wants *everyone* to be with him forever.

THE GOOD SAMARITAN

The goal of our relationship with God is to let him into every area of our hearts so that we can experience the depths of the love that he has for us. The image that often comes to mind when I think about the human experience of letting God love us is the parable of the Good Samaritan (see Luke 10:25-37). When Jesus told this story to his followers, he was answering a lawyer who questioned

---

[2]   St. Thomas Aquinas, *Summa Theologica* I-II, 26, 4.

him about the prerequisites for entering into eternal life. Jesus asked him what is written in the Law, and the man responded: to love God and one's neighbor. But the lawyer then asked whom exactly he should consider his neighbor. Jesus responded with a parable.

In his story, Jesus tells of a man who was traveling from Jerusalem to Jericho. As he made his journey, a group of robbers stripped him, beat him, and left him half dead. As the man lay on the side of the road, a priest and a Levite passed by him without attending to his needs. Later, a Samaritan was passing by. He saw the stripped, beaten, half dead man on the side of the road—and he had compassion on the man. He went to him, tended to his wounds, took him to an inn, and continued to take care of him. Finally, this good Samaritan entrusted the man to the innkeeper, assuring him that he would come back for him.

Clearly, this parable shows how Jesus enters into our wounds and entrusts us to the community of the Church until he comes again at the end of time. The half-dead man represents all of us who allow Jesus to enter our brokenness and wounds. The man who was stripped and beaten by robbers could have resisted the help of the Samaritan. In order for the Samaritan to help him, he had to touch the man. The physical touch of another when we have bodily wounds can hurt. Sometimes, we would rather remain wounded than allow another into our pain. The wounded man experienced healing not only because the Good Samaritan entered his wounds, but also because he allowed the Good Samaritan to enter his wounds.

Pray

A Conversation with Jesus

After spending some time meditating on the message the Scripture passage said to me, I will then bring it to Jesus. My prayer goes something like this:

"Lord, first I want to apologize for all of the times that I tried to do things my own way. I'm sorry for the ways that I have not surrendered to the promptings of your Holy Spirit in my walk toward eternity. Please give me the grace that I need to be more docile to your love. Thank you for the times that I was able to be obedient. In the depths of my heart, I know that true fulfillment only comes from being submissive to your will, your ways, and your time. Amen."

Contemplate

Sitting with and Gazing at God

During my period of contemplation, I sit silently in the presence of God in the Eucharist. I dwell on the face of Christ that I encountered during my time of reading, meditation, and prayer.

Act

Reading, Meditating, Praying, and Contemplating – and Now Acting

In the *The Bible Timeline: The Story of Salvation,* presenter Jeff Cavins invites his audience to "get a Bible, get away, and get together with God." To cultivate a deeper intimacy with God, I look at my calendar and find an entire day that I can set aside to be with God in the Scriptures. I let my family and friends know that I will be taking a "desert day" and will be unavailable. That day, I turn off the television and WiFi and put away my smartphone and laptop. I spend the entire day reading the Scriptures, meditating on God's Word, praying with my Lord, and resting with him in the silence of my heart.

In fact, this is what the apostles did throughout their three-year walk with Jesus—they lived in and with the Word made Flesh. Abandoning lifelong friends and family, they journeyed with Jesus on the water, in the mountains, and in the Garden of Gethsemane. After the Resurrection, they continued to spend time alone with Jesus away from the distractions of the world, as they preached and ministered to the Church, as they were imprisoned and martyred for their witness, in imitation of their Savior.

Invitation to
PRAYER

To cultivate a deeper intimacy with God that is rooted in the Bible, I encourage you to spend time with Jesus through the practice of *lectio divina*. Here, I recommend the parable of the Prodigal Son (Luke 15:11-24):

> There was a man who had two sons; and the younger of them said to his father, "Father, give me the share of property that falls to me." And he divided his living between them. Not many days later, the younger son gathered all he had and took his journey into a far country, and there he squandered his property in loose living. And when he had spent everything, a great famine arose in that country, and he began to be in want. So he went and joined himself to one of the citizens of that country, who sent him into his fields to feed swine. And he would gladly have fed on the pods that the swine ate; and no one gave him anything. But when he came to himself, he said, "How many of my father's hired servants have bread enough and to spare, but I perish here with hunger! I will arise and go to my father, and I will say to him, 'Father, I have sinned against heaven and before you; I am no longer worthy to be called your son; treat me as one of your hired servants.'"
>
> And he rose and came to his father. But while he was yet a distance, his father saw him and had compassion, and ran and embraced him and kissed him. And the son said to him, "Father, I have sinned against heaven and before you; I am no longer worthy to be called your son." But the father said to his servants, "Bring quickly the best robe, and put it on him; and put a ring on his hand, and shoes on his feet; and bring the

fatted calf and kill it, and let us eat and make merry; for this my son was dead, and is alive again; he was lost, and is found."

Now, apply the five steps of *lectio divina* to this passage.

1. **Read:** What does the particular biblical text say in and of itself?

2. **Meditate:** What does this passage "say" to you?

3. **Pray:** Converse with the Holy Spirit about what you have meditated upon.

4. **Contemplate:** Allow yourself to experience the gaze of Jesus as you look at him.

5. **Act:** What concrete action can you take in your daily life in response to what you have read, meditated, prayed, and contemplated.

? QUESTIONS
For Meditation and Discussion

1. Would you say that you know a lot about God? Would you say that you know him?

2. St. Teresa of Calcutta often asked her sisters, "Have you seen with the eyes of your soul how he looks at you with love? Do you really know the living Jesus, not just from books but from being with him in your heart? Have you heard the loving words he speaks to you?" How do you spend time cultivating a living and vital relationship with Jesus?

3. To really hear God in prayer requires active listening. What does active listening mean to you? How would you describe having an open heart and mind?

4. Have you ever experienced God's love in prayer? How?

5. How might you pray with the Bible to know Jesus better and open yourself to hearing his voice?

6. Have you ever experienced Jesus standing at the door knocking? If so, were you able to open up and let him into the "messy" areas of your heart?

7. Do you ever "beat yourself up" because of your ongoing battle with sin? Do you believe God loves you unconditionally?

8. Love means willing the good of the other. What is the good God wills for you?

9. Are you open to letting God into every area of your life? Are you open to letting him in every area of your heart so that you can more fully experience his love for you?

10. Are you open to incorporating *lectio divina* into your prayer life?

Chapter Five

Breaking the Chains of Sin

Late one night, I was talking with a good friend of mine, Fr. Kurt, and I made the comment, "Man, I love Jesus so much! I just want to be a saint so bad!" Fr. Kurt looked at me intently and asked, "Do you?" I said, "Yeah, of course I do!" He then sucker-punched me with a follow-up question: "If you really want to be a saint, then why don't you show in your actions what you say with your words?" "What do you mean?" I asked. He responded, "I think that when a person loves someone else, they make tangible sacrifices to safeguard their relationship. I honestly think you could be making a little more of an effort in your actions to show Jesus how much you love him." These words cut me deep in my heart because I knew that I loved God and he loved me. I really thought I had been living out my love for God. As I later prayed about my friend's challenging words, the Lord showed me that my actions do not always reveal my desire to be a saint.

The thing is, even after we experience the infinite and intimate love of God, we still struggle with our vices, which are those bad habits that we have done over time and seem to have control over us. After we encounter the love of God, one of the graces we receive is that we no longer desire to sin; but unfortunately, desire is not enough. As St. John Paul II said, becoming aware of our sinfulness is only the *starting point* of virtue. Much work still needs to be done. I can *desire* to be physically fit, but if I stay on my couch, eating potato chips and watching television for hours every day, I will remain flabby and unfit.

TRADING VICE FOR VIRTUE

How can we replace our vices—our bad habits—with virtues, or good habits? We need to cooperate with God's grace. God can (and does) work miracles in our lives. God wants us to experience freedom! Typically, though, we need to cooperate with his grace to be truly free in our walk with him. The wedding feast of Cana offers an example of this process. During the celebration, when the wine ran out, Mary went to the servants and told them, "Do whatever he [Jesus] tells you." The servants went to Jesus. He told them to fill the jugs with water, and they obeyed him. The servants filled the water jugs to the brim. After they cooperated with Jesus and participated in his task, he transformed the water into wine (John 2:1-12).

First, we need to reflect on those vices we struggle with the most—and then actively combat them by seeking to cultivate their opposing virtues. For example, as for many, lust was one of the dominant vices in my life when I was younger. Lust can be defined as the bad habit of seeing others as sexual objects for our own pleasure. Even after I encountered the love of God at retreats, in the confessional, in spiritual direction, and in my daily times of prayer, I still struggled with this vice for years.

When I was able to see the hold the vice of lust had on me, I began to take action by cultivating the virtue that directly opposes it—temperance. Temperance is the virtue by which we deny ourselves sensible pleasures through habitual moderation.[1]

Since lust concerns inordinate pleasure, I began to pay attention to other things in my life—things that were good—from which I derived pleasure. After praying about this, I decided to deny myself even legitimate pleasure from these things on a consistent basis. My hope was that by denying myself pleasure in non-sinful things, I would eventually be able to deny myself pleasure from sinful vices as well.

My first act of self-denial concerned the time I spent in the shower. I enjoy taking long, hot showers. I usually can listen to an entire album and sing every song while taking a shower. After college, when I would visit my parents' house, they would know when I was home because they could hear me in the shower, singing at the top of my lungs. My dad would remark to my mom, "Honey, do you hear that? It sounds like a dog is dying in the bathroom!" So I began to limit the amount of time I spent in the shower. Instead of jamming out to an entire album, I only listened to a few songs.

After a while, I not only denied myself the pleasure of taking long, hot showers, I also began to take cold showers. During Lent one year, a bunch of my friends came up with the idea that we should all make a communal sacrifice of taking cold showers, offering them up for all the women we had hurt in our lives. I thought this was a great idea. I took my first cold shower on Ash Wednesday and the next day. I found these extremely uncomfortable! So by Friday, I was back to taking hot showers. So much for my "communal sacrifice." Soon, though, I began to take my desire to grow in virtue seriously, and I began taking cold showers at least two days a week.

---

[1]   Jordan Aumann, O.P., *Spiritual Theology* (London: Bloomsberry Continuum, 2017), 297.

Next, I applied this method of self-denial to food. In the beginning, I cultivated temperance by eating three meals a day without adding any salt and pepper (which I really enjoy). I also would intentionally choose salad dressings I did not like. In this way, I still ate three meals a day, but I was not eating for the sake of pleasure. To be clear: Pleasure in itself is not bad, but when trying to fight against particular vices, it is helpful to avoid the pleasure in good things.

Eventually, I began to reduce the number of meals I ate every day. Instead of three full meals, I would only eat two very small portions for breakfast and lunch and one normal-sized portion for dinner. After I became accustomed to this kind of fast, I began experimenting with eating only bread and water on certain days. I was not starving myself, but I was reducing the pleasure I normally got from eating. Again, this was done to help me live the virtue of temperance by denying myself pleasure from good things so that I could overcome the vice of lust in my life.

Finally, I applied temperance to music. I think it's pretty clear how much I enjoy music. I sing in the shower, in the car, when I am working out, and even when I pray. In confession, a priest once gave me a penance of not singing for an entire day. This was one of the most difficult penances I have ever received! After cultivating temperance with the shower and food, I began to deny myself the pleasure of music a few days a week. I began by limiting how much music I listened to on a given day. At first, I drove to school every morning in silence. I would only listen to music on my drive back home in the afternoon. After a while, I picked two days a week to deny myself music, both listening and singing, for the entire day. While this was very difficult for me, I am sure everyone around me was extremely grateful!

When we fast from good things, it is helpful to fill the emptiness with Jesus. A practical way to invite Jesus into our fasting is by

praying the Rosary, the ancient prayer that Mary, the mother of
Jesus, has invited us to pray in all of her apparitions.

APPARITIONS: MORE THAN JUST "SEEING THINGS"

Speaking of apparitions, let's talk about exactly what an
apparition is. An apparition is an appearance on earth of an angel,
holy person, or canonized saint, most commonly the Blessed
Virgin Mary, with a message from God. In the Bible, there are
many accounts of apparitions.

In the Old Testament, God sent an angel to appear to Abraham to
stop him from sacrificing his son Isaac (see Genesis 22). He also
sent two angels to communicate with and protect Lot, Abraham's
nephew, and his family, as God prepared to destroy Sodom and
Gomorrah for their wickedness (see Genesis 19:1-29).

In the New Testament, both Mary and St. Joseph experienced
apparitions of an angel who communicated God's will that Mary
become the mother of Jesus, the incarnate Son of God (see Luke
1:26-38; Matthew 1:20-21). At the Transfiguration, Moses and
Elijah—though both had died more than a thousand years before
the birth of Christ—appeared with Jesus on the top of Mount
Tabor (see Matthew 17:1-8; Mark 9:2-8; Luke 9:28-36). This was
possible because "nothing can separate us from the love of God,"
not even death (Romans 8:38-39).

When our loved ones pass away to the next life, they remain
united to us through Jesus! When a person is a member of the
Church, they remain a part of it, even in heaven. So if a particular
Christian helps us grow closer to God in this life, when they die,
they continue to draw us to Jesus because we are united to them
through him.

Just as there were apparitions in biblical times, apparitions
continue to occur in our own day throughout the world,
particularly those of the Blessed Virgin Mary. Since the sixteenth

century, Mary has appeared in Guadalupe, Mexico; Lourdes, France; Fatima, Portugal; Kibeho, Africa; among many other places. In each of these apparitions, Mary proclaims a similar message: Enter into a deeper relationship with her Son, Jesus, through penance, the Eucharist, and by praying the Rosary.

Several years ago, I went on pilgrimage to Lourdes, one of the most famous and visited Marian apparition sites. There, in 1858, Mary appeared to a young girl Bernadette Soubirous. As I prayed at the Grotto where Mary appeared, I was struck for the first time that Our Lady had appeared on earth to invite people to have a deeper faith in Jesus.

THE POWER OF THE ROSARY

I often read books from wise men and women on how to grow in our relationship with God. These learned people offer various methods and forms of prayer. However, the "method" of Mary, the mother of Jesus, as shared in her appearances on earth, is simple: "Pray the Rosary."

You may have heard of the Rosary growing up. You may have even prayed it as a child, or you may pray it today. But many Catholics, unfortunately, are unfamiliar with this traditional and powerful prayer. So what exactly is the Rosary? In his letter *Rosarium Virginis Mariae* ("The Rosary of the Virgin Mary"), St. John Paul II writes, "The Rosary, is at heart a Christocentric prayer … the Christian people sit at the school of Mary and are led to contemplate the beauty of the face of Christ and to experience the depths of his love."[2] In a nutshell, the Rosary contains the principal events of the life of Christ.[3]

When we pray the Rosary, we gaze at and meditate on the face of Jesus, just as Mary gazed on his face from the time of his birth to his death, then on his resurrected face, and now on his gloried

[2] St. John Paul II, Apostolic Letter *Rosarium Virginis Mariae* (2002), 1.
[3] Ibid., 2.

face in heaven. As St. John Paul II says, "To recite the Rosary is nothing other than to contemplate with Mary the face of Christ."[4] As we meditate on the Person of Jesus, we ask Mary to intercede for us as she interceded for the people at the wedding of Cana, by praying the Hail Mary. Just as we often ask others to pray for us, in the Rosary, we ask Mary to pray for us to know Jesus as intimately as she does. *(For a practical guide on how to pray the Rosary, please see page 163 of the appendix.)*

The fruit of contemplating the face of Christ in our thoughts and imagination is that we begin to manifest Jesus in our words and actions. Our words and actions flow directly from our thoughts and imagination. So if we pray with our imagination, then our mind will become a sacred place and our intimacy with Jesus will show itself in how we speak and act with our family, friends, neighbors, and coworkers.

By spending time consistently meditating on the life of Jesus and denying myself legitimate pleasures, I became capable of denying myself the pleasure I derived from lust, when I objectified others in my thoughts, words, and actions. Through my faithful cultivation of the virtue of temperance, by the grace of God, I found the freedom to love others by denying myself.

As I began to experience freedom from the vice of lust, I became aware of another vice that was dominant in my life. (You may also have this experience in your walk with Jesus—that is, you address one vice only to discover another that you had been unaware of. Do not be discouraged! There is always room for us to grow in virtue on this side of heaven.)

ENVY AND PADRE PIO

The new dominant vice of which I became aware was envy. This is "sadness at the sight of another's good and immoderate desire

---
[4] Ibid., 3.

to acquire them for oneself, even unjustly" (CCC 2539). Envy is an extremely serious vice because it was through the envy of the devil that sin and death entered the world (see CCC 413).

I can vividly recall a time in my priesthood when I was envious in my thoughts. In the months leading up to my ordination, two of my friends invited me to go with them on a pilgrimage to Italy. We would travel to Rome, Assisi, and San Giovanni Rotondo. I was ecstatic. These were places where some of my favorite saints had lived and ministered for years: The remains of St. John Paul II and St. John XXIII were in Rome, and the relics of St. Francis and St. Claire were in Assisi. The city I most anticipated visiting, though, was San Giovanni Rotondo, where the incorruptible body of St. Pio of Pietrelcina (Padre Pio) was located.

St. Pio was a Franciscan friar who died in 1968. His life was far from typical in that he experienced many extraordinary miracles throughout his ministry. Shortly after being ordained to the priesthood, he received the stigmata, the five wounds of Jesus, on his body. For fifty years, he had the stigmata; his wounds were healed only shortly before his death. In addition to the marks of Christ on his body, he also experienced such mystical phenomena as levitation (i.e., bodily elevation while praying), bilocation (i.e., appearing in two different locations at the same time), and the ability to read souls (i.e., helping people expose their hearts to the mercy of Jesus in the confessional). Years after he passed away, his body was exhumed and found to be incorruptible—that is, without any natural decay—and has remained so to this day. His corpse looks exactly the same now as it did on the day he died.

My mother had a great devotion to Padre Pio when I was growing up. His pictures and relics could be found throughout our house. Though I questioned the goodness of the Catholic Church when I was young, I could never get Padre Pio out of my head. My mother regularly asked him to intercede with Jesus for our family, so I am certain his intercession led me to the youth conference that changed the course of my life. So I could not wait to go to San Giovanni Rotondo to visit the incorruptible body of Padre Pio and celebrate Mass on the same altar he did. I looked forward to thanking him for his intercession with Jesus for my ongoing conversion.

Several months before our trip, I reached out to a mutual friend who worked at the shrine where Padre Pio's body laid. He assured me that he would set aside a time for me and my friends to celebrate Mass on the same altar on which Padre Pio celebrated daily Mass.

Before traveling to San Giovanni Rotondo, we spent a few days praying in the different churches in Rome. As I knelt down in the chapel dedicated to St. John Paul II, I perceived God speaking to me. He said, "Josh, you will receive the gift if it is for your sanctification. If it is not for your sanctification, you will not receive the gift." When I heard these words, I questioned whether they were truly from God or from my own imagination. I immediately wrote them in my journal, resolving to return to them later for further discernment. I set my journal aside and focused again on Jesus in the Blessed Sacrament.

The next day we left Rome and began our journey to Padre Pio's shrine. I spent the hours of the trip anticipating what it would be like to celebrate Mass on the same altar as Padre Pio. Upon arriving at the shrine, though, our guide informed us that he was ill and would be going home. As a result, we would not be able to celebrate Mass on Padre Pio's altar after all! I was too upset even to respond. When one of my friends informed the guide that we had scheduled a time to say Mass, he simply reiterated that he wasn't feeling well and walked away.

Disheartened by this news, we walked toward the sacristy to figure out what our next move was going to be. As we were discussing the matter, a young Italian priest walked into the sacristy and greeted us warmly. He told us that he, too, had been ordained recently, and that he was there to celebrate Mass on Padre Pio's altar. I was overcome with sadness and thought, "If I can't say Mass on Padre Pio's altar, then he shouldn't be able to either!" I would soon come to see that the sadness I was feeling was really due to envy.

Overcome with disappointment, I walked outside to get a breath of fresh air. I decided to go visit Padre Pio's incorruptible body on display in the lower church. I vividly remember walking up to his corpse and, like a spoiled child having a tantrum, saying, "Padre Pio, you've been praying for me my whole life. Are you seriously going to let me come all the way here and not celebrate Mass in the chapel where you grew to intimacy with Jesus?!"

Wrapped in envy, I stood silently in the presence of Padre Pio's body. Then I heard the same words from the day before at St. John Paul II's chapel: "Josh, you will receive the gift if it is for your sanctification. You will not receive the gift if it is not for your sanctification." I immediately realized that maybe I did not have to celebrate Mass on Padre Pio's altar after all. Maybe this had nothing to do with becoming holy. Perhaps the newly ordained priest from Rome had received this gift because he needed it in his journey to becoming a saint. I apologized to our Lord for my envious reaction to another person's blessing. When I went back to the sacristy, I joined my friends in asking the young Italian priest if we could concelebrate Mass with him, and he graciously welcomed us.

Upon leaving the shrine, I recalled Jesus' words to Peter in John's Gospel about not focusing on what God is doing in the lives of others. After Jesus invited Peter to feed his lambs and tend his sheep, he indicated how he would be called to serve him in the future:

> Jesus said to him, "Truly, truly, I say to you, when you were young, you girded yourself and walked where you would; but when you are old, you will stretch out your hands, and another will gird you and carry you where you do not wish to go." This he said to show by what death he was to glorify God. And after this he said to him, "Follow me" (John 21:18-19).

Wow! Jesus just told Peter how he was going to die. Imagine how you would feel if Jesus said similar words to you?

How does Peter respond to this breathtaking news? Amazingly, he takes his eyes off of Jesus and focuses his attention on one of the other disciples. He asks Jesus, "Lord, what about this man?" Jesus turns to Peter and says, "If it is my will that he remain until I come, what is that to you? Follow me" (John 21:21, 22).

Peter was so focused on the other disciple that he wasn't able to reflect on Jesus' words about his future martyrdom for the Lord. He had a lot of rich spiritual food to digest, but he instead chose to dwell on someone else's faith journey. Aren't many of us like Peter at times? That is, worrying about what God is doing in the lives of others. We fall into the trap of comparing ourselves to them. A quote attributed to President Theodore Roosevelt says it well: "Comparison is the thief of joy."

God had given me a huge gift with a free pilgrimage to Rome, Assisi, and San Giovanni Rotondo. Instead of dwelling on God's gifts to another, I should have been grateful for his many gifts to me. My joy was robbed in that moment by comparing my gifts with a gift given to another … and envying it.

At times, we can fall into the trap of eating the bitter fruit of the tree of envy. To avoid this unnecessary misery, we should fast from dwelling on the lives of others and comparing ours to theirs. Rather, we should offer prayers of gratitude to God for the gifts he has given us … and pray that God bestow even more gifts on those with whom we have felt envious. As we eradicate the vice of envy and its power over us, we can see clearly that God has already given us (and everyone else) what we need to be saints.

KEEP THE FOCUS ON GOD … AND HIS GIFTS

Here is a practical and effective tool on how to fast from involving ourselves in other people's lives: We can limit our interaction with social media—or, better yet, eliminate it altogether from our lives. Through social media, so many have become obsessed by—and envious of—what they perceive as others doing better than them. Of course, these impressions are usually not totally based in reality; there is a certain amount of illusion that others create with social media, to put "their best foot forward." Denying ourselves an unhealthy focus on social media can free us from much misdirected envy and allow us to focus more on God's goodness to us, on the blessings he has given us.

Gratitude can have a powerful effect on our lives. A practical way to focus on the many gifts God has given each of us in our lives is to pray the "Litany of Gratitude." In this prayer, we ask God to shine his light on our minds and hearts to help us be grateful for his blessings. In his Examen Prayer, St. Ignatius of Loyola prescribes gratitude as the first step: "To give thanks to God our Lord for the favors received."[5] We all have received—and continue to receive—a variety of gifts from God every day. These gifts can range from simple to extraordinary. After reflecting on your many gifts, write five to ten of them on a sheet of paper and then thank God for each one.

---

[5]   St. Ignatius of Loyola, *The Spiritual Exercises of St. Ignatius,* trans. Louis J. Puhl (New York: Vintage Books, 2000), no. 43.

Here is an example:

1. **_The gift of being able to walk:_** _Heavenly Father, thank you for allowing me to walk. I am aware that so many people throughout the world do not have this gift. Clearly, since you have given me the gift of being able-bodied, you desire that I use this gift responsibly to aid in my relationship with you and my community._

2. **_The gift of being able to read:_** _Heavenly Father, thank you for the gift of my education. I recognize that so many people in the world do not have access to good schools. Because of the schools I attended as a youth, I am able to read the Bible, your inspired Word. This gift has enabled me to know your Son, Jesus, in a profound way._

3. **_The gift of being able to participate in Mass:_** _Heavenly Father, thank you for allowing me to be able to attend Mass every day. I know that many Christians are persecuted all over the world and are not allowed to publicly participate in the Eucharist. The presence of Jesus in the Eucharist is a gift I hope I will never take for granted._

4. **_The gift of being able to receive the sacrament of reconciliation:_** _Heavenly Father, thank you for allowing me to experience your mercy. Every day, I fall short in my thoughts, words, and actions. The forgiveness you offer me in this sacrament is a daily reminder that I am called to forgive others who offend me in thoughts, words, and actions._

5. **_The gift of being loved by God:_** _Heavenly Father, thank you for loving me in the midst of all of my mess. I recognize that_

my community can be messy as well, and I hope to be able imitate you in loving them in the midst of their brokenness.

After spending some time being thankful for the Lord's goodness toward us, we can then ask God to deliver us from any potentially self-indulgent and destructive appetites. After retiring from his post as secretary of state to St. Pius X, Cardinal Merry del Val composed a famous prayer known as the "Litany of Humility" (see the following page). In my own life, I have found it helpful to recite this prayer for people of whom I have been envious. As I recite the prayer, I replace the word "other" with a person's name. Instead of brooding on what he has that I do not have, I pray for him to have more if it will help him get to heaven. At the same time, I pray for the grace to desire less, recognizing that I have already received the greatest of gifts in Jesus' unconditional love for me.

The Litany of Humility

O Jesus, meek and humble of heart,
Make my heart like yours.

From self-will, deliver me, O Lord.

From the desire of being esteemed, deliver me, O Lord.
From the desire of being loved, deliver me, O Lord.
From the desire of being extolled, deliver me, O Lord.
From the desire of being honored, deliver me, O Lord.
From the desire of being praised, deliver me, O Lord.
From the desire of being preferred to others, deliver me, O Lord.
From the desire of being consulted, deliver me, O Lord.
From the desire of being approved, deliver me, O Lord.
From the desire to be understood, deliver me, O Lord.
From the desire to be visited, deliver me, O Lord.

From the fear of being humiliated, deliver me, O Lord.
From the fear of being despised, deliver me, O Lord.
From the fear of suffering rebukes, deliver me, O Lord.
From the fear of being calumniated, deliver me, O Lord.
From the fear of being forgotten, deliver me, O Lord.
From the fear of being ridiculed, deliver me, O Lord.
From the fear of being suspected, deliver me, O Lord.
From the fear of being wronged, deliver me, O Lord.
From the fear of being abandoned, deliver me, O Lord.
From the fear of being refused, deliver me, O Lord.

That others may be loved more than I,
Lord, grant me the grace to desire it.
That, in the opinion of the world, others may increase and I
*   may decrease,*
Lord, grant me the grace to desire it.

That others may be chosen and I set aside,
Lord, grant me the grace to desire it.
That others may be praised and I go unnoticed,
Lord, grant me the grace to desire it.
That others may be preferred to me in everything,
Lord, grant me the grace to desire it.
That others may become holier than I, provided that I may
become as holy as I should,
Lord, grant me the grace to desire it.

At being unknown and poor,
Lord, I want to rejoice.
At being deprived of the natural perfections of body and mind,
Lord, I want to rejoice.
When people do not think of me,
Lord, I want to rejoice.
When they assign to me the meanest tasks,
Lord, I want to rejoice.
When they do not even deign to make use of me,
Lord, I want to rejoice.
When they never ask my opinion,
Lord, I want to rejoice.
When they leave me at the lowest place,
Lord, I want to rejoice.
When they blame me in season and out of season,
Lord, I want to rejoice.

Blessed are those who suffer persecution for justice's sake,
For theirs is the kingdom of heaven.

Along with cultivating the virtues of temperance, gratitude, and humility, I continued to grow in my experience of freedom from enslavement to bad habits through frequently immersing myself in the sacrament of reconciliation. This powerful sacrament was given to the Church by Jesus after his resurrection. As St. John writes:

> Jesus said to them again, "Peace be with you. As the Father has sent me, even so I send you." And when he had said this, he breathed on them, and said to them, "Receive the Holy Spirit. If you forgive the sins of any, they are forgiven; if you retain the sins of any, they are retained" (John 20:21-23).

In the sacrament of reconciliation, God forgives our sins through the ministry of the apostles' successors, the bishops of the Church, and their collaborators, priests. So bishops and priests can forgive our sins in the sacrament of reconciliation because of the authority given to the apostles by Christ himself (see CCC 1461). After confessing our sins, and right before we are absolved from them, we are asked to recite some words that show our sorrow for our sins—that is, an "act of contrition." I usually use the traditional form of the Act of Contrition:

> *O my God, I am heartily sorry for having offended you. I detest all of my sins because of your just punishment, but most of all because I have offended you, my God, who are all good and worthy of all of my love. I firmly resolve with the help of your grace to do my penance, avoid the near occasion of sin, and to sin no more. Amen.*

When we pray the same prayers over and over again, we can begin to miss their profound meaning. There was one line in the Act of Contrition that I never focused too much on: "I firmly resolve with the help of your grace to *avoid the near occasion of sin.*" I didn't really think about what it means to avoid the "near occasion" of sin. In my seminary studies, I learned that the original Latin word in the Act of Contrition that we translate as "avoid" is *fugiturum.* Literally, though, this word means *flee*—that is, run away as quickly as possible—from the near occasion of sin.

The desert Fathers of the early Church clearly understood the need to "flee" from the people, places, and activities that were near occasions of sin for them. Many of these great early saints who fled to the wilderness did not do so because they were prudes or to escape or because they couldn't "cut it" in the real world. They did so because they honestly recognized their limitations and weaknesses with sin and sought to remove as many near occasions from their lives as possible.

To flee from near occasions of sin is perfectly in line with the Scriptures. Consider the birth of Jesus, when the three wise men followed the star to visit and worship the new King at the manger in Bethlehem. After they had come and paid homage to the infant Jesus, they were warned in a dream not to go back to Herod and report where the Lord had been born. They saw that Herod's motives were not pure. So they returned to their country by another route to avoid Herod entirely (see Matthew 2:1-12).

A NEAR OCCASION EXAMINED

One of my good friends, Christopher, encountered Jesus for the first time in high school. After graduating, he decided to follow in the footsteps of his parents and siblings and attend Louisiana State University (or LSU). When he was accepted to LSU, his next big decision was whether to join a fraternity. He had heard about the fraternity lifestyle from his father: excessive drinking and casual sex of the hookup culture. He was confident, though, that his experience would be different, as he had a solid prayer life and a good support system of fellow believers.

So Christopher decided to join a fraternity after all. He began his frat life by remaining in a fairly virtuous state, and he even witnessed Christ to his fraternity brothers. The party atmosphere of the frat house, though, ultimately proved irresistible. While he remained on the "straight and narrow" outside the fraternity environment, he found himself falling prey to all the negative behavior he had promised himself he would avoid.

He was very conflicted, and he shared his struggles with me. After he had told me about his fraternity experiences, I told Christopher, "It sounds to me like your near occasion of sin here might not be alcohol or your fraternity brothers. It might be simply attending the parties at your frat house." He looked at me, confused. "Really?" I went on, "Yes. If you are able to participate in meetings, study, and hang out at the frat house with your friends and not behave foolishly, then the house is not your near occasion of sin. If you are able to tailgate before football games, go to dances, and even hang out at bars with your fraternity brothers without getting drunk, then clearly partying itself is not your near occasion of sin. However, if every time you party at the fraternity house, you get wasted and treat women as objects, then these parties are your true near occasions of sin and should be avoided." I challenged him on whether he could avoid these frat house parties, and he reluctantly said that he could. To his surprise, he discovered that when he avoided parties at the frat house, he neither objectified women nor abused alcohol.

My friend Christopher's experience illustrates an important aspect of overcoming our vices: We need to avoid the people, places, and activities that are not conducive for our walk toward eternity—and may actually keep us bound in a particular bad habit.

In our walk toward true freedom in Christ, we might relapse into our old vices. Though we may overcome a particular vice

by practicing its opposite virtue, temptations will still come …
but do not lose hope! Even if we make great progress in virtue,
concupiscence remains very real. (Remember that *concupiscence*
is a disordered inclination toward sin we all inherit from our first
parents.) So we will still be tempted, and we may even fall. But
we must not become discouraged! Discouragement is not of God.

EVEN SAINTS BATTLED VICES …

We should take encouragement from the fact that even the
greatest saints struggled with overcoming vice. St. Augustine
struggled with lust, St. Francis de Sales with wrath, and
St. John XXIII with sloth. A notable saint who struggled for years
with her dominant vice was Teresa of Avila.

St. Teresa of Avila was a sixteenth-century Spanish Carmelite
nun, who was later declared a Doctor of the Church because
of her profound insights into the spiritual life. Like many of us,
St. Teresa had a "past." She was a popular girl in her youth. She
frequented the best parties and participated in the juiciest gossip.
Many men were infatuated with her, and she was infatuated with
her own image. Her father, seeing his daughter's many defects,
sent her away to a boarding school to safeguard her from what he
perceived were her near occasions of sin. Away from her comfort
zone of parties, gossip, and men, she became attracted to the
religious life. Though her father disapproved, she still chose to
respond to her calling, and she joined the Carmelite order at the
age of twenty.

Though she had become a cloistered Carmelite nun, this did not
immediately make Teresa holy. Like many of us, she still had not
yet opened all the areas of her life that needed purification to the
Lord. As such, she continued to desire the attention, admiration,
approval, and affection of those she interacted with as a nun. As
she admits, "I delighted in being thought well of."

At the core of her heart was an internal struggle. She wanted to be holy. She wanted to be faithful to God. She wanted to serve her neighbor. At the same time, though, she wanted to be liked. She wanted to be comfortable and to have others think well of her. Finally, after nearly twenty years of this struggle, she experienced a freedom from her dominant vices through the grace of God in her prayer, fasting, and avoidance of the near occasions that had led her away from fulfillment in the Lord.[6]

It is important to recognize that it took St. Teresa of Avila decades to find freedom from her vices. Some of us like to put timetables on when we will no longer struggle with a particular sin. But this is not healthy or realistic. We need to trust that God is at work in our lives through his grace and is working with us in our desire to overcome our vices. We can have an intentional relationship with Jesus Christ and still struggle with a particular sin. The key word here is *struggle.* The task is to never give up the fight in our walk toward eternity.

Think about athletes. If they want to grow in their abilities, they need to spend a lot of time and effort nurturing their physical gifts—through training, practicing, and exercising. Athletes do the same workouts over and over again. They experience pain and suffering in their efforts, particularly at first. Over time, though, they are able to work out with ease. The greatest athletes, the superstars and record-holders, did not give up when their training became difficult.

We have been created to be much more than good athletes. We have been created by God to be saints. We have been created to run a race with a finish line that is literally beyond this world. To finish this race, all we need to do is keep trying. St. Paul's experience should encourage us: "I have fought the good fight, I have finished the race, I have kept the faith" (2 Timothy 4:7).

6   Colleen Carroll Campbell, *My Sisters the Saints: A Spiritual Memoir* (New York: Image, 2012), 14-17.

Invitation to
PRAYER

As we strive to overcome our vices with virtues, it is important for us to examine our consciences at the end of the day to discover how we are doing. Spiritual writers recommend that we do this examination at the end of the day, perhaps right before we go to bed.

The Bible can be a helpful lens through which to examine our conscience. For example, if we are struggling with loving others, St. Paul's words to the Corinthians give us an idea of what we need to do:

> Love is patient and kind; love is not jealous or boastful; it is not arrogant or rude. Love does not insist on its own way; it is not irritable or resentful; it does not rejoice at wrong, but rejoices in the right (1 Corinthians 13:4-6).

We have been created by a God who is Love, "to love and be loved." Here, I invite you to reflect on this passage from 1 Corinthians and ask God to show you where you need to grow in this virtue. To help this reflection be more fruitful, replace the word "love" with your name.

[YOUR NAME] is patient. *Jesus, have I been patient with you today? Have I been frustrated with your timing in answering my prayers? Have I been patient with my own growth in virtue, or have I been frustrated with my lack of growth? Have I been patient with others?*

[YOUR NAME] is kind. Jesus have I been kind toward you today? Have I been kind to my family, classmates, co-workers, neighbors, and friends? Have I been gentle with the drunkards and homeless in my community?

[YOUR NAME] is not jealous. Jesus, have I gotten upset when I see the way that you are working in the lives of others? Have I intentionally prayed for others to experience joy in their relationships and work even when I am experiencing sorrow?

[YOUR NAME] is not boastful. Jesus, have I sought too much attention from others in my community through my posts on social media? Do I always make sure people notice my good works every day?

[YOUR NAME] is not arrogant. Jesus, do I recognize my own limitations? Did I say "yes" too many times today? Have I done more than I am capable of doing well?

[YOUR NAME] is not rude. Jesus, have I gossiped about others today? Have I spoken rudely to others at the supermarket, at school, on the road, or at the office?

[YOUR NAME] does not insist on (his/her) own way. Jesus, have I been open to doing things your way? Do I always have to have the last word in disagreements?

[YOUR NAME] is not irritable. Jesus, have I been short-tempered lately? Have I been too sensitive? Have I gotten irritated when little things did not work out as I expected?

[YOUR NAME] is not resentful. Jesus, in prayer, have I focused on the offenses of others more than I have on your face? Have I dwelled on past wounds? Have I shared the forgiveness I have received from you with others?

[YOUR NAME] does not rejoice at wrong. Jesus, am I happy at others' mistakes, particularly people I don't like? Have I celebrated bad behavior?

[YOUR NAME] rejoices in the right. Jesus, do I acknowledge that I am nothing without you? Am I grateful for your teachings?

QUESTIONS

For Meditation and Discussion

1. What dominant vice are you struggling with? Are you open to combating this vice with its opposing virtue?

2. Are you open to continuing this practice as other vices reveal themselves?

3. How has fasting—not just from food, but from other legitimate pleasures—helped you overcome particular vices? How has it helped you draw closer to Jesus?

4. Have you experienced the power of the Rosary? If so, how?

5. What people are near occasions of sin for you?

6. What places are near occasions of sin for you?

7. What activities are near occasions of sin for you?

8. What is your dominant fault in this season of your life?

9. What virtue could you seek to grow in more intentionally?

10. Do you fast outside of Lent? If not, what are some practical things you can "fast" from that will help you spend more time with God?

Chapter Six

Reforming Community from Within

As we continue to deepen our relationship with Jesus, opening ourselves to his love in the midst of our mess and cultivating virtue in our walk toward eternity, the inevitable happens: The Church presents us with a bunch of rules to follow. Some of these rules are of divine origin, while others are not. The way these rules are presented to us can make them a bridge or a barrier.

In my second year of theological studies at Notre Dame Seminary, I was given the opportunity to teach St. John Paul II's Theology of the Body to juniors at St. Mary's Academy in New Orleans. St. Mary's is an all-female Catholic high school with a high percentage of non-Catholic students, mostly from various Protestant backgrounds. This was an exciting time for me, as I got to witness my students' enthusiasm every week as they learned about John Paul's teaching, which helped them to understand the gift of who they are and why God created them.

In the second semester, we transitioned from teaching the Theology of the Body to apologetics, which is basically a course on the teachings of the Church. To my surprise, I encountered a lot of resistance from the students when I began presenting this topic. So I asked them why. One of the young ladies responded, "I just don't like the Catholic Church because it has too many rules!" I said, "Yes, I agree. The Catholic Church does have a lot of rules. Are there any particular rules that you find problematic?" She replied, "Well, for one, the Church doesn't allow divorced people to get remarried."

This student had hit upon one of the most controversial and challenging of the Church's "rules." As a priest, I hear often from people who have been told things about the Church's teaching on divorce that are simply wrong. For instance, they were told by nuns, deacons, and catechists that no divorced person can receive the Eucharist—which is not true. What the Church teaches is a divorced person cannot remarry if their former spouse is still living. If a divorced person enters into marriage without receiving an annulment, then he or she is asked not to receive Holy Communion. Why? Because, by their actions, they are not in communion with the teachings of Christ and his Church.

I asked the young lady, "So your main issue with the Catholic Church is its teaching that people who are divorced cannot get remarried?" "Yep," she responded. A few other students agreed, saying, "That's right!" I responded, "OK, cool. What about Jesus? How do you all feel about him?" They all exclaimed, "We love Jesus!"

They followed up with, "Yeah, we just don't like the Catholic religion because its rules are too strict!" Continuing our dialogue, I said, "So you don't like the Catholic Church because it is too strict with its rules, specifically about divorce, but you do love Jesus, right?" "Yep," the majority of the class again exclaimed. I then asked them, "Since you love Jesus, are you willing to listen to what he says about divorce?" "Of course," they responded. I invited them to open up their copies of the Bible to the Gospel of Matthew where Jesus said, "Whoever divorces his wife except for fornication and marries another woman commits adultery" (Matthew 19:9).

I continued, "When Jesus said these words, his disciples struggled with this teaching. They said, 'If such is the case of a man with his wife, it is not expedient to marry' (Matthew 19:10). Notice that Jesus didn't say, 'Sorry, guys. Let me change my teaching to make you more comfortable.' Though Jesus' disciples struggled with many of his 'rules,' at least initially, they remained in relationship with him. Over time, they were able to understand and accept his teachings."

After the students and I read the passage from Matthew, the room went silent. One of the girls finally spoke up, "That's crazy. I've never heard that verse before." I informed the students, "The thing about the Catholic Church's 'rules'—the Church doesn't just make them up. Everything the Church teaches she has received from Jesus and is sharing his teachings with the world. The question is *why* Jesus teaches that divorced people cannot get remarried while their former spouse is still living. The reason is that the marital bond is a sign that points us to Jesus' relationship with the Church. As St. Paul wrote to the Ephesians, 'Husbands, love your wives, as Christ loved the church and gave himself up for her' (Ephesians 5:25). Marriage, then, is an image of Jesus, the Bridegroom, and the Church, his Bride. Since Jesus will never leave the Church for another bride, a husband and wife cannot leave each other either for other spouses if they entered into a valid covenant with each other."

I invited the students to recall what we learned from St. John Paul II the previous semester in his Theology of the Body. We had studied the four marks of Christ's love for the Church—his love is *free, total, faithful,* and *fruitful.*

Free

No one forced Jesus to suffer and die on the Cross. As Jesus says, "I lay down my life, that I may take it again. No one takes it from me, but I lay it down, and I have power to take it again" (John 10:17-18). He makes it clear that he permitted Judas to betray him, the guards to arrest him, the priests to attack him, and the soldiers to beat and crucify him. As the divine Son of God, Jesus could have stopped them at any moment, but he freely chose to suffer for the salvation of humanity.

Likewise, for a couple to enter into a valid marriage, they must imitate Jesus and do so freely. If either party is being coerced into marriage or does not have the capacity to marry (for various reasons), then the marriage is not valid in the eyes of God.

Total

Jesus gave everything for the Church; he held nothing back. Not only was he crucified, he allowed his heart to be pierced so that his blood and water could flow out of his side (see John 19:34). Similarly, when a man and woman get married, they are called to love each other totally as well, intending at the moment of their consent to hold nothing back from each other.

Faithful

Though Jesus was encouraged to come down from the Cross, he did not. The soldier taunted him, "If you are the King of the Jews, save yourself!" (John 23:37). But Jesus remained resolute in his fidelity to the will of the Father to suffer and die for his Bride, the Church. In marriage, both spouses declare their intention to be faithful to each other for the rest of their lives, no matter what.

Fruitful

The fruitfulness of Christ's death on the Cross, by reconciling sinful humanity to God, is the opening of the gates of heaven. So eternal life with God is the fruit of Jesus' passion. In marriage, a couple declares their intention to be open to receiving children, whether they be biological, adopted, or spiritual.

Whenever we perceive rules as coming between us and a relationship with Jesus Christ, we instinctively rebel. When I reoriented the conversation back to Jesus and his intimate love, though, the students expressed a newfound openness to this particular "rule" of the Church. When we can see how a particular teaching actually helps us grow closer to Jesus, then it is easier to accept.

CIARA'S STORY

This was the case with a young woman named Ciara whom I was blessed to accompany in her relationship with Jesus and the Church. Her first three years at LSU were spent attending class, working at off-campus internships, and partying on the weekends with her closest friends. By the start of her senior year, Ciara had not been to Mass in four years. When she returned to school after summer break, the last thing she expected was to spend any time at the Catholic Student Center.

Returning to campus was different that year, though. It turned out that her closest friends had all encountered Jesus over the summer through our small-group Bible studies. All of them were more interested in their new faith in Christ than they were in partying.

Like most of us, Ciara had really enjoyed being a part of a community. Though she couldn't relate to her friends' newfound faith, she was not willing to stop spending time with them. They invited her to join them at Mass, Eucharistic Adoration, praise and worship nights, small-group Bible studies, retreats, conferences, and service opportunities. She reluctantly joined them because she would rather be part of a community of "Jesus freaks" than be part of none at all.

Eventually, she scheduled an appointment with me to vent why she was so upset with her friends' faith renewal. She shared, "Father, I don't know how to say this without offending you, but I haven't been to Church since I began college four years ago. I stopped coming because the lifestyle I've been living goes against everything I was taught growing up as a Catholic. I think the Church is behind the times and closed-minded, and I disagree with its positions on many moral issues. Now, all of my closest friends want to spend most of their time here at the Catholic Student Center. Father, I didn't know this Student Center even existed until a few months ago. What am I supposed to do? I don't want to lose my friends, but I just don't feel comfortable here."

Pondering how to best respond to Ciara's dilemma, I offered these words: "Wow, Ciara, thank you so much for sharing your heart with me. It sounds like this transition your friends are going through is really difficult for you. But I also hear how much you love your friends, and I'm sure they love you, too. You shared that it is difficult for you to be here, but I'm sure your presence means a lot to your friends. To be honest with you, I enjoy seeing you as well! I would love for you to continue joining us for Mass, Eucharistic Adoration, Bible study, and all the other things going on here. You don't need to change your moral positions or your approach to God and the Church. Just know that you are always welcome here."

I am happy to report that Ciara took me up on my offer and joined us at different events throughout the following week, both at the center and on campus. Occasionally, she would come and remind me that she still wasn't sorry for her moral choices, and I would thank her for sharing and invite her to continue spending time at the Catholic Center.

After about eight months, Ciara asked me if we could schedule an appointment to meet. As she sat in my office, I perceived that there was something different about her. She was no longer confrontational and she seemed excited to talk with me. She began to relate how spending so much time in Adoration, praise and worship, and group Bible study had made her open to having a personal relationship with Jesus.

Though she was ready to be in a relationship with Jesus, she said that she still did not believe all of his teachings. This reminded me of Jesus' first disciples, who did not believe Jesus when he told them to "eat his body" and "drink his blood" during the Bread of Life discourse (see John 6). After Jesus told them that they needed to consume his flesh and drink his blood to have eternal life, many of his disciples immediately stopped following him. (see John 6:66).

Unlike those disciples of Jesus who walked away from him when they found his teachings too difficult, Ciara continued to spend time with him. Eventually, due to her love for Jesus, she had the courage to acknowledge that she still did not fully understand all of his teachings. Nonetheless, she believed in Jesus, so she decided to accept the Church's teachings on faith and morals. Once Ciara decided to follow Jesus and live in conformity with the Church's moral teachings, she experienced a joy that surpassed her wildest dreams.

Like Ciara, I know many people who don't fully understand—or accept—the teachings of the Church. If you are one who does not trust the Catholic Church, I would encourage you to trust Jesus! If you aren't spending intentional time with Jesus in Adoration of the Blessed Sacrament and reading the Bible, then I invite you to begin making these activities a part of your schedule. Apart from an intentional relationship with Jesus, the teachings of the Church do not make sense. On the other hand, if we "lean into" Jesus, he will give us the grace to believe even those teachings that are difficult to accept.

To be painfully honest, often what is proposed by the Church is not well-articulated by her teachers. As with the students I taught at St. Mary's, the Church's teachings are then mistakenly seen as unjust, arbitrary, and made up by her leaders. Worse yet, some teachers actually pass on views that are not truly the teachings of Christ. What do we do in this situation?

Let me offer the experience of a good friend from childhood, Alicia, who stopped going to Mass in high school. After my ordination, Alicia reached out to me and told me she wanted to reestablish her relationship with God and come back to the Catholic Church. I was so excited for her, and I could not wait to get her "plugged into" a new relationship with Jesus through his Church.

After a few years of walking with Jesus and his Church as an intentional disciple, she enrolled her son, my godson, into a Catholic school. Though her son would be one of the school's few biracial students, Alicia did not anticipate that this would be an issue. To her surprise, the school's administration immediately had a problem with him. He was sent home with a "write-up" slip for violating the hair grooming policy prescribed in the school handbook.

Concerned, Alicia called me, as there seemed to be nothing out of the ordinary about her son's hair. True, the texture of his hair was naturally more curly and thicker than those of the school's white students. She took him to a barber in an attempt to have his hair cut so that it would conform with the school's hair policy. Amazingly, he was again sent home with a "write-up" indicating that he was still in violation of the school policy. Now his mother and I were both upset—especially since his hairstyle was the same as mine! I immediately wanted to call the school and have a conversation with the principal about discrimination. Before I did, though, I decided to take my frustrations to Jesus first so that he could help me order my thoughts and words.

One of my spiritual directors during my seminary formation, Monsignor William Fitzgerald, had frequently reminded me to communicate with Jesus before I communicated with people. He lived this in his own life by refusing to answer the phone the first time anyone called, allowing all calls to go straight to voicemail. When a caller received his voicemail, the caller would hear, "You've reached Monsignor Fitz! I want you to know that you are very important to me, and so is your reason for calling. But I want you to know, if you have not spent time talking to Jesus about whatever it is you want to talk with me about, it would be best for you to hang up the phone right now, pray, and then call me back after you have gone to Jesus first! God bless you and I cannot wait to hear from you!"

One of the ways Monsignor Fitz taught me to pray was using a method called **ARRR,** which is an acronym for **A**cknowledge, **R**elate, **R**eceive, and **R**espond. When communicating with Jesus, he invites us to do the following:

1.   **A**cknowledge our thoughts, feelings, and desires.

2.   **R**elate our thoughts, feelings, and desires to our Lord.

3. Receive from the Lord by spending time with him in the Sacred Scriptures.

4. Respond to his Word with a concrete action.

During my time before the Blessed Sacrament, I acknowledged that I was upset that my godson was being discriminated against because of the texture of his hair. I related my frustrations to Jesus in the Eucharist. Then, I opened up the Sacred Scriptures to receive wisdom from our Lord on how he wanted me to proceed. The passage that I received was the story of Queen Esther in the Old Testament (see the book of Esther).

Esther was a Jewish orphan living in the Persian Empire. She was very beautiful. At the time she entered adulthood, the Persian king Ahasuerus sent out a decree for all the young virgins in the kingdom to be gathered before him so that he could choose his next queen. After spending time with Esther, the king desired her above every other woman he encountered, so he put on her the queen's diadem.

As queen, Esther had the privilege of being part of the king's inner circle. Upon discovering that one of the king's right-hand men had plans to annihilate the Jewish people, she turned to prayer and fasting. She then used her privilege as queen to enter the king's courts and inform him that one of his confidants had plans to kill her people.

The king listened to his queen and saved the Jewish people from being annihilated. Her people were saved because Esther used her queenship to protect them when they did not have the capacity to protect themselves.

After reading and praying about the story of Queen Esther, I responded to my godson's hair discrimination by writing a letter to the principal of his school. I wrote this letter from my privileged role as a diocesan priest and as co-chair of the Commission on Racial Harmony of the Diocese of Baton Rouge.

In my letter, I sought to communicate my frustration by using a method called "Facts, Feelings, and Future." In this method, the concrete details of a situation are communicated first, followed by a description of how the situation has made the writer feel and a proposal for a different outcome in the future. In my message to the principal, I addressed how my godson had been written up because the texture of his hair cannot be cut in accordance with the rules of the school—which I noted is a ministry of the diocese we both served. I then expressed my feelings of frustration by the injustice of this handbook policy. Finally, I invited her to reconsider my godson's "write-ups" as well as the rule that enabled him to be punished for being ethnically different.

A few days after I sent my letter, Alicia received an apology from the principal about her son's recent "write-ups." Unfortunately, though, the school did not revise its hair policy. So what would be an appropriate response to such a decision? Should we revolt because certain members of the Church are unwilling to reform unjust rules? Or should we stay in relationship with the Church and propose reformation of unjust policies? I propose the latter. If we walk away from the community of Christ, then we lose the opportunity to help things change for the better—and then others in the future will not benefit from our fidelity to the cause.

In our walk with the Church, God may call us to be his instruments in helping "reform" the attitudes and actions of our brothers and sisters, even those in Church leadership. In some cases, we may witness the fruits of our fidelity to our broken communities.

This was the case with St. Catherine of Siena (1347–1380). In the year 1309, as a result of political disorder and the influence of the French king, Philip, Pope Clement V moved the papal court from

Rome to Avignon in France. For the next seventy years, the popes would reside in France rather than in Rome. This situation was scandalous to Catholics of the time because it appeared that the popes were nothing but tools of the king of France.

St. Catherine grew up with the pope living in France. In prayer, the Lord began to inspire her with the courage to confront Pope Gregory XI and encourage him to return to Rome, the rightful place for the pope to reside as successor of the apostle Peter. For three months, Catherine unceasingly communicated her desire to the pope that he serve Jesus and his Church from the seat that had been set apart for him in Rome. Initially, Gregory XI resisted her request, but because of her persistence, he finally returned to Rome in 1377. Catherine lived to see the fruits of her fidelity to God's will.

Many other saints, though, did not see the fruit of their efforts in their lifetimes as St. Catherine did. Because they persevered in their relationship with the Church and those who were doing it harm, they witnessed the fruits of their efforts from heaven. Such was the case with Blessed Elizabeth Leseur (1866–1914). Elizabeth's husband, Felix, was a French medical doctor who had a deep-seated hatred for the Catholic Church. Though Felix was raised Catholic, he had left the Church as a young adult and later served as the editor of an atheistic journal. In her early thirties, Elizabeth had an interior conversion to Christ and became deeply rooted in her Catholic faith. When she became intentional in her walk with Jesus and the Church, she consistently began to pray for the conversion of her husband. Eventually, she was diagnosed with cancer and died in her late forties.

Although Blessed Elizabeth prayed for the conversion of her husband every day, she did not see the fruit of her prayers in her lifetime. After she died, though, Felix found her letters, including one written to him. This note inspired him to visit Lourdes, France, where the Blessed Virgin Mary had appeared in 1858. During his stay in Lourdes, he underwent a conversion and became a believer in Christ. He would eventually be ordained a Catholic priest, and he spent the rest of his life traveling and speaking about the devotion of his wife, who never gave up praying for his conversion. Though Elizabeth did not see the fruit of her prayers in her lifetime, her perseverance certainly bore fruit in her husband's conversion and the service he provided for the Church of twentieth century.

Similarly, Blessed Charles de Foucauld (1858–1916) experienced supernatural fruit that benefited many after his death. Charles was orphaned as a child and rejected Jesus and the Catholic Church as a teenager. He engaged in an adulterous relationship that led to his dismissal from the army. Later, though, Charles became acquainted with devout Jews and Muslims whose faith in God inspired him to return to his Catholic faith. Eventually, after spending intentional time with Jesus, he felt called to enter the religious community of Trappist Monks.

Though he ended up leaving the monastery after a few years, he perceived God's call to become a priest. After he was ordained, he was inspired to establish a religious community in Africa to offer hospitality to Christians, Muslims, Jews, and people of no religious background. He once wrote, "The love of God, the love for one's neighbor ... All religion is found there ... How to get to that point? Not in a day since it is perfection itself: it is the goal we must always aim for, which we must unceasingly try to reach and that we will only attain in heaven." Shortly after he wrote these words, Charles was shot to death by bandits in northern Africa. After his passing, five religious communities, associations, and institutes were established based on his spirituality. While Blessed Charles did not live to see the fruit that is still changing lives, in heaven he certainly is witnessing the fruit of his many years of fidelity.

If you are experiencing situations where members of the Church have established rules that are not producing good fruit, please do not give up on them. The lives of St. Catherine of Siena, Blessed Elizabeth Leseur, and Blessed Charles Foucauld witness to the change that God can bring about if we simply persevere in relationship with those we find difficult. We might just be the instruments God wants to use to transform hearts, minds, and policies. Since God never gives up on us, how can we in good conscience give up on each other? We need to be open to meeting people where they are and trust that the Holy Spirit will find ways to help us connect with them in our walk together toward eternity.

It is helpful to remember that the apostles of Jesus did not always agree with each other, but they remained in relationship. Before his passion, Jesus was walking with the apostles toward Jerusalem. Shortly after he told them that he would die and rise from the dead, James and John asked Jesus if they could receive places of honor in the kingdom. After the other apostles heard this, they were understandably angry toward James and John (see Mark 10:32-41). Though they were unhappy with James and John, they did not leave them behind. They remained in relationship with them.

Later, at Jesus' crucifixion, the only apostle who showed up at the foot of the Cross was St. John, the Beloved Disciple. After Jesus' death, John did not reject the other apostles because they had abandoned Christ. He went back to where they were hiding behind closed doors and dwelled with them (see John 20:19-22).

After the Ascension and Pentecost, the apostles still made mistakes and had disagreements, but they remained in relationship with each other, honestly communicating their thoughts and strongly held beliefs. We can see this in the interactions of St. Paul and St. Peter. After the coming of the Holy Spirit at Pentecost, Peter, the chief apostle, was "on fire" for Jesus. He was filled with the Holy Spirit, and his preaching led to the conversion of thousands to Christ (see Acts 2:41). Though he was filled with the Holy Spirit and had been chosen by Jesus to lead the Church, Peter was still an imperfect human being who made mistakes that hurt others who were trying to grow in their relationship with Jesus.

In the Acts of the Apostles, we read how Peter ate with Gentiles (i.e., non-Jews), which many Jews who had converted to Christianity found scandalous because Gentiles did not observe the dietary prescriptions of the Law.[1] The Jewish Christians challenged Peter, asking him, "Why did you go to uncircumcised men and eat with them?" (Acts 11:3). Peter defended his association with Gentile Christians by saying that he had received a vision from God inviting him to partake in foods that were once considered unclean with people who were once considered outsiders. He made it clear to the Jewish Christians that there should be no distinction between believers, whether they were of Jewish or Gentile background (see Acts 11:1-18).

At some point, though, Peter became a bit hypocritical on this issue. Due to "peer pressure" from some of James' disciples, he began to withdraw from the Gentile Christians with whom he had freely associated. Not only did he separate himself from them, he also began to impose rules on them based on the old dietary prescriptions of the Law. So, when Paul became aware of the division these man-made rules were causing in the community, he confronted Peter and forcefully communicated his disappointment: "If you, though a Jew, live like a Gentile and not like a Jew, how can you compel Gentiles to live like Jews?" (Galatians 2:14). In his letter to the Galatians, Paul reminds Peter that Jesus Christ has freed us from the works of the Law, which includes the necessity of circumcision and the obligation to follow the dietary laws of the Old Testament. Such laws divide the Jewish and Gentile believers, whereas in Christ, all are one (see Galatians 3).

---

[1]   Frank Mater, *Sacra Pagina: Galatians* (Collegeville, MN: Liturgical Press, 2007), 85.

Here, we need to recognize something that is vitally important. Though Paul challenged Peter for wrongfully imposing man-made rules on the Gentile Christians, he did not break communion with him. He did not walk away and start his own Church, nor did he walk away from his relationship with Christ because of Peter's mistake. Paul recognized that, even though he did not agree with Peter's decisions, he still needed to be in communion with him. Likewise, Peter knew that he needed Paul. They understood that they both had been called by Christ and were necessary members of the Church. Likewise, we need the Church, and the Church needs us. Each of us has received particular gifts and talents from the Holy Spirit that we need to share with each other. If we leave, then the body of Christ is incomplete.

One of my favorite passages is from St. Paul's first letter to the Corinthians. Here, he addresses the different members of the body of Christ and their dependence on each other in their walk toward eternity:

> For just as the body is one and has many members, and all the members of the body, though many, are one body, so it is with Christ. For by one Spirit, we were all baptized into one body … For the body does not consist of one member but of many. If the foot should say, "Because I am not a hand, I do not belong to the body," that would not make it any less a part of the body. And if the ear should say, "Because I am not an eye, I do not belong to the body," that would not make it any less a part of the body. If the whole body were an eye, where would be the hearing? If the whole body were an ear, where would be the sense of smell? But as it is, God arranged the organs of the body, each one of them, as he chose. If all were a single organ, where would the body be? As it is, there are many parts, yet one body. The eye cannot say to the hand, "I have no need of

you," nor again the head to the feet, "I have no need of you" (1 Corinthians 12:12-21).

Notice how St. Paul emphasizes that we all need one other. No person is an island. Just because we are different and sometimes disagree does not mean that we should isolate ourselves from other members of Christ's Church. The Church needs all of us, in communion with one another, sharing the gifts we have been given to build up the body of Christ. At times, we may be unhappy with how leaders in the Church present Christ's teachings or establish "bad," man-made rules that seem unjust, but we should not separate ourselves from them. The Church needs us ... and we need the Church.

If we want to have a personal relationship with Jesus, whose love fulfills the deepest desires of our hearts, then we need to have a relationship with his Church. It really can't be just "Jesus and me." We cannot separate Jesus from his people. Remember that St. Paul, before his conversion experience, persecuted Christians. As we have seen, Jesus does not ask him, "Why are you persecuting my Church?" but rather, "Why do you persecute me?" (Acts 9:4). He directly identifies himself with the members of his Church. On the Cross, Jesus, the Bridegroom, gave himself eternally to the Church, his Bride—and what God has joined together, no man can separate. There is no such thing as Jesus without his Church. We cannot take Jesus without his people. The Church and Jesus are a package.

Quite often, I reflect on the ways in which I have offended God throughout my life. Time and time again, Jesus has invited me back into relationship with him. God has never given up on me, and he will never give up on you. This is why we love God so much! How can we claim to love God, whom we cannot see, if we do not love the broken members of the body of Christ, whom we can see?

Invitation to
PRAYER

As you spend time with God in prayer, I want to invite you to practice the **ARRR** method. Again, this method of prayer is an acronym for **A**cknowledge, **R**elate, **R**eceive, and **R**espond. When communicating with Jesus, I invite you to do the following:

1.   **A**cknowledge your thoughts, feelings, and desires.

2.   **R**elate your thoughts, feelings, and desires to our Lord.

3.   **R**eceive from our Lord by spending time with him in the Sacred Scriptures.

4.   **R**espond to his Word with a concrete action.

QUESTIONS
For Meditation and Discussion

1. What teachings of the Church do you find particularly
    challenging? Why might growing into a deeper
    relationship with Jesus help resolve these challenges?

2. How do you respond to members of the Church that
    enforce man-made rules that are harmful to the body
    of Christ?

3. Are you sometimes unsure of the appropriate response
    when you are in conflict with a member of the Church?
    What could you do to discern the best course of action?

4. Have you ever wanted to revolt against the Church
    because certain leaders are unwilling to reform "broken"
    rules? Why might staying in communion with the Church
    be the better course?

5. Do you believe you are an essential part of the body of
    Christ, the Church? What particular gifts do you believe
    you have that can be of service to the Church?

Chapter Seven

Prioritizing Prayer

Every year, I go on a silent retreat to spend some "alone time" with Jesus. Similarly to the way married couples go on annual vacations to nurture their relationships, most priests, monks, friars, and nuns go on "vacations with Jesus" in yearly weeklong retreats. Several years ago, not long after I was ordained, I was preparing for my annual retreat, and I received a surprising message. A religious brother I knew had just made the choice to leave religious life.

At the conclusion of the retreat, I reached out to this brother to see how he was doing. He shared with me some insights that I will forever hold and reverence in my heart. "Josh," he said. "When I was in formation with my religious community, we had a structured schedule of specific times for prayer, study, work, socializing, and resting. When I began serving in a parish, however, things changed completely. It was not a question of my dedication. Without realizing it, I began to set prayer aside so that I could spend more time ministering to my parishioners. From early morning until late at night, all of my time was devoted to serving their needs—from developing new programs, to thinking of new ways to facilitate their encounters with Jesus and helping them experience the Church in her truest sense. It became a well-intentioned but vicious spiral—the more I worked, the less I prayed; and the less I prayed, the more frustration I began to experience in my vocation, and I began to feel a deep longing for something else ... for someone else."

Clearly, when he prioritized his intimate encounters with Jesus in prayer, he was content in his state of life and zealous in his work for the Lord. Yet when he decreased his intentional, consistent time with Jesus in prayer, he became frustrated with his calling and began to look outside his relationship with Jesus and the Church for fulfillment. Our conversation prompted me to make a resolution to never allow anything or anyone to get between me and my time with Jesus. Somewhat ironically, however, not long after I made this resolution, I, too, began to experience burnout from too much work and not enough prayer.

THE "SAYING 'YES' TO EVERYTHING TRAP"

Shortly after my ordination, I was assigned to a thriving parish in the city of Baton Rouge. The parishioners there were hungry for the Lord, and I was ready to serve them and help them grow closer to Jesus. There were so many needs, and I had the best intentions to help as many people as I could. Every day, I would make myself available to hear confession and to bring the anointing of the sick to people in hospitals and in their homes. I also began offering spiritual direction for any parishioners who wanted to grow into a deeper intimacy with Jesus Christ, and I offered pastoral counseling to any who needed guidance, were grieving, or had marital challenges. Added to all this was a decision to teach theology classes. So you could say I was a "24/7 priest": I was always available to the needs of my parishioners. At this point, my time spent in prayer had not decreased, but it did begin to change quite a bit. Rather than dwelling on God's love for me and my love for God, I spent most of my time in prayer discerning how I could best serve those who came to me for ministry and offering prayers of intercession for them.

After I began to see much supernatural fruit in the parish, other people in my diocese began to reach out to me for assistance in their work for the Lord. First, an order of nuns, a number of married couples, and quite a few young adults asked me to accompany them through spiritual direction. I thought, *How can I say no to these people who want to grow in their relationship with the Lord?* So, of course, I agreed.

Then I received an invitation from a local Catholic media apostolate to start a new radio show that would appeal to black Catholics and young adults. Since I believed the Church should do much more to minister to black Catholics and young adults, I quickly jumped onboard for this project as well.

During this time, I also began getting a lot of requests from the predominantly black churches of my diocese. When I was ordained in May of 2014, I was the only African American priest in my entire diocese. An African American once told me that when her sons saw my picture in the local paper, they were shocked to see a black priest. One of them said, "Mom, I didn't know that black people could become priests!" I completely identified with this remark because I had thought the exact same thing as a child. Every opportunity I got, I made a special effort to be a good role model to young people and certainly to those in the predominantly black parishes.

Not surprisingly, perhaps, the more time I spent fulfilling all these needs and requests, the less time I spent in intimate prayer with Jesus. In fact, my personal prayer became filled with unnecessary distractions and was becoming shorter all the time. Ministry had become so overwhelming that I decided to stop taking a day off each week so I could meet the needs of all the people who were reaching out to me.

I vividly remember going to bed every night with a migraine headache and waking up every morning feeling totally exhausted. When I first was ordained, I looked forward to waking up every morning to spend some intentional time with Jesus. I simply could not wait to visit with Jesus in prayer. But in this new season of being a 24/7 priest, my first thought in the morning was, "Dang, another day." I knew that the second I got to my office, I would be bombarded with voicemails, emails, and unexpected visitors asking for my increasingly limited time. The joy I had once experienced in my priesthood was slowly fading away.

Even though I was doing good work for Jesus and the Church, I was not abiding in relationship with him, and I was losing my peace. As St. Teresa of Calcutta once said:

> The devil very often tempts the good with good things, so that good people, distracted by things they should not be doing, compromise the few good things they should be doing. So instead of doing what they have been called to do well, they do many good things God never asked them to do poorly.[1]

DOING VERSUS BEING

Although we connect overworked, stressful lifestyles with today's fast-moving world, this tendency is not isolated to the twenty-first century. The Gospel of Luke tells us how Jesus went to visit his close friends Mary and Martha, who had invited him to spend time with them in their home. Jesus began to teach, and Mary sat at his feet listening to his words. Meanwhile, Martha was busy doing a lot of work—good work, seemingly necessary work—for her guest. Eventually, Martha complained to Jesus, saying, "Lord, do you not care that my sister has left me to serve alone? Tell

[1]   Mother Teresa, *Where There Is Love, There Is God* (New York: Image, 2012).

her to help me." The Lord responded to Martha's complaint with words that penetrate my heart daily: "Martha, Martha, you are anxious and troubled about many things; one thing is needful. Mary has chosen the good portion, which shall not be taken away from her" (Luke 10:40, 41-42).

Clearly, Jesus was not suggesting to Martha that her work was unimportant. What he was indicating, however, is that Mary chose the "better part" because she spent time with Jesus, sat at his feet, and listened to his words before she did anything else. She did not try to serve Jesus in the way she thought best; rather, she went to him first. As she sat at Jesus' feet, she opened herself up to hearing his voice and doing what he was calling her to do at that moment. Martha, on the other hand, did not go to Jesus first. She did a lot of good things for Jesus, but they were all good things that he had never asked her to do. So she was distracted in her life, frustrated with her sister, and anxious in her relationship with God. Now, like Martha, here I was doing too much, which had led me to being distracted in prayer, frustrated with those I was serving, and anxious about things over which I had no control.

Since I was now aware that I had a problem, I made an emergency appointment with my spiritual director, Fr. Vic. On my way over to meet him, I called one of my best friends, Fr. Andrew Merrick, to vent my struggles to him. After I had finished, he said, "Josh, if you needed to make an appointment with the best doctor in the city, would you expect him to meet with you the same day you called for an appointment, or do you think you might need to wait a few weeks before he could see you?" I said, "I would probably expect to wait a few weeks to meet with him." He said, "Exactly. So tell me, why are you saying yes to everybody who calls you and agreeing to put them on your calendar as soon as possible? Why don't you ask them to wait a few days or a week so you can prioritize your time with Jesus in prayer?" His words pierced me to the heart.

Shortly after this call had ended, I arrived at St. Joseph's Abbey to visit Fr. Vic. After I relayed to him my conversation with Fr. Andrew, he surprised me by asking the same exact question. I was blown away. I now knew that the Holy Spirit was communicating to me through these two holy men. I needed to better discern the things I was doing so that I could safeguard my time of intimate prayer with our Lord.

To paraphrase an insight of St. Thomas Aquinas, virtuous people keep themselves within their own bounds. In other words, we all need to accept our necessary but limited role in the body of Christ. I used to believe that since I had so many people to minister to, that I simply did not have time to pray well. But this was a lie. I had created this need to serve as many people as possible—that is, to accept immediately every invitation and request—because I did not have order in my life. God was not asking me to extend myself to everyone who requested my time; that was my decision. I discovered that I needed boundaries so I could better discern how Jesus was calling me to serve him as a priest.

As we get more plugged in to our communities, all of us are going to be confronted with the many needs of our fellow parishioners. In his book *The Purpose Driven Life,* evangelical pastor Rick Warren presents three practical questions that we can use to discover the limited ways we are being called to serve the Church:

1.   Is this invitation important and urgent?

2.   Is this invitation important but not urgent?

3.   Is this invitation not important and not urgent?[2]

Depending on one's season of life, certain things may be important and urgent now that were not important and urgent years ago and vice versa. For instance, now that I am a priest, it is always important and urgent for me to be available to people for the

---

2   Rick Warren, *The Purpose Drive Life: What On Earth Am I Here For?* (Grand Rapids, MI: Zondervan, 2002).

anointing of the sick. If I receive a call at three in the morning after a long day's work, I will certainly not be passionate about getting up to anoint someone. However, I will prioritize this invitation because only priests have been given the sacramental authority to "bind and loose" and anoint the sick, an authority I received on the day of my ordination. Therefore, this invitation is always important and urgent.

An invitation that may be important but not urgent for me is counseling a college student who is experiencing heartache from a recent romantic breakup. Based on my experience as a campus minister at LSU, college-age people break up all the time! Certainly, anyone going through the end of a relationship is in pain, and though I have compassion for such suffering, it is definitely not that urgent. Meeting with me can wait. In the past, when a student came to me in this situation, I would meet with him or her immediately, which could have potentially taken me away from other more pressing needs. Once I realized that a number of other counselors were available to help hurting students, I began to ask those requesting to see me to wait a couple of weeks. Happily, more often than not, by the time the student and I would meet, he or she would have already moved on from the breakup.

Another invitation I received that was unimportant and not urgent was calling out the winner of bingo at the local senior citizens club. Any person can perform this task. Unless the task is life-giving for me, I should delegate it and not lose sleep over not being available.

Obviously, activities that are important and urgent are different for everyone. However, it is important to keep things in perspective. For example, a young working mom of three small children might see a special on television about children who are starving in another country and in need of full-time missionaries. Are missionaries an urgent need? Yes! But is it important and urgent for a mother of three small children to respond by becoming a full-time missionary? No! Such a decision would actually take her away from her primary vocation as a mother. However, if this same mom is nursing her child, waking up at a three in the morning to nurse her baby is both important and urgent.

Not long ago, a good friend of mine asked for advice on discerning the direction he should go in his life. He had recently undergone a profound conversion and gave up his former life as a rapper. He got married, became a father, and began working a nine-to-five job. Though he no longer rapped in the streets, every now and then he would use his gift of rap to inspire youth not to go down the same wayward path he had lived for so many years.

At one of my friend's rare performances, he encountered a guy who managed Christian rap artists and who offered him a deal to tour for six months spreading the Word of God. It is certainly important and urgent for our youth who are going down the path of drugs and gangs to be inspired by reformed rappers. My friend certainly had the gifts to be used as an instrument to inspire. However, he was married with several small children. If he went on tour, who would take care of his family? Would his children be OK knowing that their father was ministering to other kids all over the country but not spending time with them? How would his wife feel if she had to raise three kids on her own while also working a full-time job?

I affirmed my buddy in his gift, but I discouraged him from pursuing the offer to tour. Objectively, the need to spread God's Word to youth through rap is important and urgent work. Subjectively, in this season of my friend's life, the invitation to travel and be away from his primary vocation as a husband and father was not important or urgent.

PRAYER: ALWAYS IMPORTANT AND URGENT

The activities we hold to be important and urgent will vary at different seasons of our lives. The one activity, though, that always remains important and urgent for each of us is prayer.

Some of us think we are too busy to pray, that we just can't find the time for prayer in our hectic lives. St. Teresa of Calcutta would respond, "If you are too busy to pray, then you are too busy." It is important for us to recognize the things we are doing but do not need to do—and stop doing them! Only then can we cultivate an interior life of prayer with our Lord.

As the *Catechism* teaches, the devil will do everything in his power to turn us away from prayer (see CCC 2725). How does he do this? By keeping us busy with unnecessary activities. One of my seminary professors, Dr. Tom Neal, once said something along the following lines: "If you want know if the devil is real, put on your calendar specific times when you will pray, and watch how many good things arise to distract you from praying." The devil seeks to distract us from prayer because he knows that prayer is where we cultivate our living and vital personal relationship with God (see CCC 2558).

In my estimation, the only way we are going to be faithful in God's invitation for us to know, love, and serve him is if we are people of prayer. When I spent time in Calcutta with the Missionaries of Charity many years ago, I heard stories from her sisters about how Mother Teresa recognized the essential importance of prayer. These sisters engage in some of the most physically draining work with the poorest of the poor throughout the world. In the early years of their work, some of her sisters wanted to reduce the amount of time they spent in prayer so they could do get more done for those in need. In response, Mother Teresa *increased* the amount of their prayer time. She recognized that the more time the sisters spent with Jesus, the more they would be able to extend their charity to the poor. As St. Teresa of Avila notes, the intensity of one's prayer life directly corresponds to the way one treats people outside of prayer.[3]

BUT WHAT *IS* PRAYER?

In reality, prayer is simple. Prayer is intentionally choosing to spend time with God. The fruit of spending time with God is this: We will begin acting like God. We really do take on the characteristics of those with whom we choose to hang around. If I spend a lot of time around friends who regularly curse and use profanity, then eventually I will be more prone to profane speech as well. If I hang out with friends who gossip, then it is likely that I will begin to gossip, too. On the other hand, if I spend time with people who are virtuous, then there is a good chance that I will begin cultivating good habits as well. If this is true with people, how much more so when we spend time with God! Simply spending time with him in prayer will change us and help us grow in holiness.

Years ago, I met a young girl who taught me the essence of prayer. Her name was Elizabeth Marie, and she was one of my parishioners. She was seven years old, and she was in and out of hospice during my time at St. Aloysius. From birth, she had experienced seizures and was unable to speak or walk. When she was able to get Elizabeth Marie out of the house, her mother would bring her to daily Mass in a wheelchair. After Mass, the two of them would spend time sitting before the Blessed Sacrament.

Since Elizabeth and her family lived down the street from the parish, I began to stop by for pastoral visits. I understood that Elizabeth Marie was the body of Christ, and during our visits, I would sit with her, hold her hand, look into her eyes, and listen to

---

[3]   Jordan Aumann, O.P., *Spiritual Theology* (London: Sheed and Ward, 1980), 316.

her attempts to communicate with me through her soft groans. I wasn't able to understand what exactly she was trying to say, but I didn't need to know.

My experience with Elizabeth Marie was similar to my experience in prayer. More often than not, when I spend intentional time with God in prayer, I sit with him, look at him in the Eucharist, hear him in the Scriptures, and listen to him speak in the silence of my heart. Similar to my experience with Elizabeth Marie, when I am with God, there are many days when I cannot perceive what exactly he is saying to me, but I am aware that he is communicating his grace to me.

How do I know this? Because we simply cannot spend any time with God without receiving his transforming grace. To use a common expression, all we have to do is "show up." Typically, the fruit of our prayer is noticed by others in our actions. Whenever I sat with Elizabeth Marie, for example, I always manifested more patience, kindness, and gentleness to others. On days when I was too busy to simply sit in her presence, I was less patient, kind, and gentle. This is even more the case when it comes to spending time with God in prayer. Those days that I prioritize intentional time with God, other people notice through my demeanor … and they also notice when I don't show up.

I would compare the power of prayer to going to the beach or hanging out on a boat for an entire day during the summer. If I simply sit on the sand at the beach or chill on a boat in the hot sun from morning to night, I will go home with either a suntan (if I used sunscreen) or a sunburn. What did I do to achieve this outcome? Nothing! I simply showed up, sat outside, and the sun did all of the work. The same is true with God. If we just show up, he will do the work! We might not *feel* his grace (like we do a sunburn), but others will *see* the grace of God at work in us by the ways we live out the virtues of Jesus toward them. Spending time in God's presence puts us in a spiritual "safe space"—a place we can feel secure in God's love for us—and the resulting grace shows itself in how we live.

The fourth-century spiritual master St. Ephrem taught, "Virtues are formed by prayer. Prayer preserves temperance. Prayer suppresses anger, prevents emotions of pride, or envy, and it draws into the soul the Holy Spirit, and raises man to heaven." Let's consider these words in light of St. Peter, with whom we have been journeying throughout this book. The Scriptures reveal two drastically different portrayals of Peter. What was the key to these two "different Peters"? Whether he was spending intentional time with God in prayer.

After Jesus instituted the Eucharist at the Last Supper, he invited the apostles to join him in the Garden of Gethsemane (see Matthew 26:36-46). He then asked Peter, James, and John to remain and watch with him as he prayed to his Father. Of course, Peter and the others consented to Jesus' request, but at some point, they chose the comfort of sleep over the task of prayer. Jesus returned from his time of deep communion with God the Father and found them sleeping. He then turned to Peter, encouraging him to pray, lest he fall into temptation. Jesus then went away again to spend time with the Father. Two more times, he returned to find the apostles sleeping. What was the fruit of Peter (and the other apostles) choosing to sleep rather than spend time with Jesus?

First, when the Temple guard came to arrest Jesus, Peter gave in to his anger, cutting off the ear of the high priest's servant. Soon after this outburst, as Jesus was led away to be questioned by the priests and elders, Peter was more concerned with the opinions of others and denied knowing Jesus three times. Then, after he denied Jesus, he cursed himself and began to swear. All of these vices flowed from one thing—his unwillingness to spend time with Jesus in prayer (see Matthew 26:69-75).

In a startling contrast to these scenes, Peter later boldly proclaimed his relationship with Jesus in the Acts of the Apostles:

> Peter, standing with the eleven, lifted up his voice and addressed them ... "Men of Israel, hear these words: Jesus of Nazareth, a man attested to you by God with mighty works and wonders and signs which God did through him in your midst, as you yourselves know—this Jesus, delivered up according to the definite plan and foreknowledge of God, you crucified and killed by the hands of lawless men. But God raised him up, having loosed the pangs of death, because it was not possible for him to be held by it" (Acts 2:14, 22-25).

How did Peter go from being filled with anger, pride, fear, and self-condemnation to fearlessly proclaiming the inclusive gospel of Jesus Christ to the people of Israel? Simple: He prayed.

In the Acts of the Apostles, we read that Peter joined together with Mary, the mother of Jesus, the other devout women, and the apostles in the Upper Room, where they were all devoted to prayer (see Acts 2:13-14). After spending days intentionally and consistently praying, Peter and those with whom he was gathered received the Holy Spirit. The Spirit, in turn, empowered Peter and the apostles to go out and boldly share the Good News of Jesus Christ. Again, all of this fruit came from intentional time spent with Jesus in prayer.

PRAYER AND THE "FIVE W'S"

Throughout this book, as we have been seeing how to walk with one another in receiving the love of Jesus in and through his Church, there has been a common thread—namely, encountering God in prayer. To help us be more intentional in our relationship with Jesus, I would like to propose a method that may be familiar to many writers and journalists: "The Five W's"—*when, where, what, who,* and *why.* This approach is not a divine mandate or a Church "rule" that we must follow. It is simply a method that works for me and that has also helped many other people in their walk toward eternity.

Every Sunday, I look at my calendar for the coming week and ask myself the following questions, each of which starts with one of the **"Five W's"**:

1. **When** will I spend intentional time with Jesus from Monday to Sunday? Once I figure this out, I pencil in the exact prayer times on my calendar.

2. **Where** will I spend this intentional time with Jesus? I then note the locations on my calendar. While the actual location does not necessarily matter, it is important to find some places where you pray consistently.

3. **What** will Jesus and I "do" together during this time? That is, what type(s) of prayers or devotions. I then pencil them in.

4. **Who** will hold me accountable for spending this time with Jesus? I then invite him or her to check in with me via email, text, call, or a personal visit.

5. **Why** am I spending this time with Jesus? We need to know why we are praying for us to be consistent and persevering in prayer.

Now, let's take a look at each of the **"Five W's"**:

When

Finding the right time to encounter God is very important. St. Bernard of Clairvaux says, "Anyone who wishes to pray must choose the right time."[4] The "right time" is different for each of us, and this time can certainly change depending on the circumstances of our lives. In the Scriptures, Jesus spent intentional time with God the Father throughout each day, in the morning, afternoon, evening, and night. So any time of day is a sacred opportunity for nurturing and sustaining our living, personal relationship with God.

In my time as a priest helping people grow in their intentional relationships with Jesus, I have had many share with me that morning is the best time for them to pray. Though not everyone is a "morning person," depending on one's state of life, morning might be the most uninterrupted time of the day. St. Bernard acknowledges that, although it is not possible for everyone, "the deep silence when others are asleep is particularly suitable for prayer."[5] When I have scheduled time for intimacy with Jesus in the afternoon, it sometimes doesn't happen because of unexpected interruptions. The same is true for night: My mind is often filled with so many distractions from the day that I can hardly focus on Jesus' love for me and the Church. Hence, if morning at all works, I would encourage you to try and spend intentional time with our Lord right after you wake up. Praying in the morning first thing can help you avoid having your prayer time interrupted—or even prevented entirely—later in the day.

I wake up every day very early to pray. When I first began getting up so early, it was a struggle. In the beginning, more often than not, I would hit the snooze button on my alarm and choose to

4   Joseph Esper, *More Saintly Solutions to Life's Common Problems* (Manchester, NH: Sophia Institute Press, 2004), 45.
5   Esper, 45.

pray later. Of course, spending any substantial time with Jesus later in the day never happened due to unexpected interruptions and distractions. To avoid hitting snooze, I decided to put my smartphone on the other side of the room so that I would have to physically get out of bed to turn it off. Once I conquered the first battle of the morning, a new one came in the form of distractions.

The battle of distractions was fought with my smartphone. After I turned my alarm off, I was instinctively drawn to check my text messages and emails. Now, my mind was filled with the distracting texts and emails, and it was very difficult to focus on what I needed to receive from God in prayer. Eventually, I made the decision not to check my messages or emails until after I had spent one-on-one time with Jesus.

Nonetheless, I still found it difficult to focus on God first thing in the morning. I began to wonder if I was trying to be a martyr about this, whether I was being too hard on myself. After all, though I was super tired, I was making an effort to spend time with Jesus. I then had an important realization: Maybe my "super" tiredness was a result of going to bed too late. When I started going to bed earlier, I found it much easier—even a joy—to wake up in the morning and spend time in prayer with Jesus.

So the first thing I would invite you to do is to look on your calendar and determine set times to pray. Again, it doesn't have to be in the morning. Though I have found morning to work well for my prayer life, all of us are different. When you discern what times are best for you to pray, write it on your calendar. Whether your prayer time is ten, fifteen, or thirty minutes—or even an hour—any consistent time spent with Jesus is time well spent. If unexpected things happen in your day that take you away from this sacred time of prayer, don't worry. The intention to prioritize Jesus on the calendar is a step in the right direction and a consolation to his heart.

Where

Regarding the importance of location for prayer, St. Bernard of Clairvaux writes, "Anyone who wishes to pray must choose the right place."[6] One of the most common places people pray is in their car or on the bus on the way to or from work. As a priest, much of my time is spent in my car, and I regularly use this time for speaking with and listening to God. Many people pray the Rosary while traveling to work or school. There are a fair amount of distractions when driving, though. After all, we need to pay attention to the road and the cars around us. So, while I recommend praying in the car or on the bus, this should not be the only place we pray if we want to cultivate a deeper, authentic intimacy with the Lord.

For some, a church or Adoration chapel might be the sacred space that is most conducive for them to encounter Jesus Christ. For others, their bedroom or living room is where they grow in intimacy with God. For still others, outside in nature—at the park, on the front porch, or in the backyard is where they find prayerful solitude with Jesus. The bottom line is this: God is everywhere, so when you discover "your" place—a place of minimal distraction that helps you grow in your relationship with God—then pencil it in on your calendar.

What

What will God and I do during our time together? It is important that we have a plan in place on our calendar for our intentional time of prayer. If we don't do this, the following can happen: We pencil in fifteen minutes of prayer beginning at six o'clock in the morning in our living room, but we don't know what or how we are going to pray, so we just sit there thinking about all the things we *could* be doing with Jesus. Then, fifteen minutes later, our intentional time is up. Because we didn't have a plan, our time in prayer was not as fruitful as it could have been.

---

[6] Esper, 45.

Without a prayer plan, we spend our time "navel gazing" or fixating on the lives of others in our world. Navel gazing is when we dwell on ourselves too much: "How well am I praying? Why haven't I been healed of this wound? Why do I still struggle with this sin? Why don't I feel anything right now?" Instead of focusing on Jesus, we make our prayer all about us. In prayer, Jesus once challenged the lay mystic Gabrielle Bossis, "Who is your God, you or I? Why don't you think of me more than of yourself?"[7] Though it is important to discuss these topics with our spiritual director, it is not possible for a lot of growth to happen in any relationship if we are only focused on ourselves.

On the other hand, our prayer can become too focused on other people (and even on places or things). Instead of actually being intimate with God, we spend our time with him dwelling on everyone else. As St. Caesarius of Arles puts it, "A person worships whatever captivates his mind during prayer. Whoever in his prayers thinks of public affairs, or the house he is building, worships them rather than God."[8]

To safeguard our prayer time with God, we need to have a plan. In each chapter of this book, we have discussed different ways of entering into a deeper intimacy with God: Adoration of the Blessed Sacrament, *lectio divina*, praying the Rosary, using the ARRR model, examination of conscience, praise and worship music, praying the Litany of Gratitude, saying the Litany of Humility, using St. Teresa of Calcutta's "I THIRST" meditation, among others. Depending on our current season of life, we sometimes will be drawn to a particular prayer or method of praying. This is normal. Simply having some kind of order in our prayer can save us from many distractions and a less than fruitful prayer time.

---

[7] Gabrielle Bossis, *He and I* (Boston: Pauline, 1969), 42.
[8] Esper, 45.

In addition to penciling in different methods of prayer, I also encourage you to leave your smartphone in the other room or at least put it in silent mode. Typically, we wouldn't be using our phones during Mass or when we are having a conversation with our significant other. Likewise, prayer is not a time when our phone should be present with its many potential distractions.

After we make our plans with the Lord, we should be open if the Holy Spirit leads us in a different direction. Our prayer plan is simply meant to help us focus on God. As St. Jane de Chantal has said:

> When the Holy Spirit has taken charge of the person who is meditating … He does with the soul as it pleases him, and all rules and methods vanish away. In the hands of God the soul must become like clay in the hands of a potter, who from it can form any sort of dish … Prayer must be carried on by grace, and not by deliberate art.[9]

With Jesus, it is always a good idea to be flexible and open to his guiding us in a new direction, much like the Holy Spirit did with the apostles at Pentecost.

Who

At the end of the day, no person is an island. We cannot live our relationship with Jesus on our own. Jesus did not call a single disciple. Rather, he called together a group of disciples to walk with each other toward eternity. We all need someone to hold us accountable. As a priest, I am accountable to my bishop. A religious sister or brother is accountable to his or her superior. A husband is accountable to his wife, and vice versa. Each of us needs someone to check on us and encourage us in our walk with the Lord.

[9] Esper, 47.

I cannot tell you how many times I have witnessed people encounter Jesus at a conference or retreat who then express a desire to have a deeper relationship with him. They do not stay true to this holy desire because they do not have anyone to check on them and hold them accountable, so they fall back to their former way of living. In the Scriptures, Nathan held King David accountable to being holy, even when he found it uncomfortable and difficult. Though being vulnerable can be difficult, I strongly encourage you to choose someone in your life who can be your "accountability partner." This person will check in with you regularly and ask you the following questions:

1. What are you currently doing for prayer?
2. How often do you pray?
3. How long do you pray each time?

Give your accountability partner permission to check on you via email, text, calls, or in person. If you are a married man, I would encourage you to invite another Christian man to be your accountability partner so that your emotional boundaries aren't crossed. Similarly, if you are a married woman, I would encourage you to invite a Christian woman to be your accountability partner.

Why

For each of us, the "why" in our relationship with God will be different. Speaking for myself, I need to pray every day so that I can abide in God's love for me. When I am not faithful to my time with Jesus, I become like the Israelites in the Old Testament and quickly forget how much God sees me, knows me, and loves me. If I am not daily receiving the love of God, then it becomes difficult for me to share his love with the often messy and broken members of his Church. I am able to give love because I receive love.

In the Gospels, Jesus performed a miracle in which he blessed five loaves of bread and two fish—and these fed five thousand people. To feed those who were hungry, Jesus "multiplied" the bread and fish and shared them with his disciples, who in turn shared them with the people (see Matthew 14:13-21). But how did such a small number of apostles manage to distribute so much food to five thousand people? They kept going back to Jesus for more. In other words, they sat at Jesus' feet and received the gift from him, and then they went to the people and shared this gift. If they had not gone to Jesus to receive the gift, they would not have anything to share with so many people who were hungry.

In this well-known miracle of the Multiplication of the Loaves and Fish, we see why it is so necessary for us to pray often and consistently. The more we receive the love of God, the more capable we are of sharing his love with others.

We know that the Church's members are broken—all of them, including you and me. Yet in the midst of our brokenness and imperfections, Jesus loves us and dwells with us. If this is how Jesus loves us, then we, his disciples, are called to bring his love to others. As we have seen, only through intentional time spent with Jesus every day is this possible.

Invitation to
PRAYER

For your time with God, I invite you to find a place that is conducive for you to be alone with him. When you determine this place, invite the Holy Spirit to inspire you with a prayer plan so that your intentional encounters with God can be fruitful. Here is how to write down the "Five W's" on your calendar for a given week:

	WHEN	WHERE	WHAT	WHO	WHY
SUN					
MON					
TUES					
WED					
THUR					
FRI					
SAT					

Do not be discouraged if the first set of "Five W's" you write down do not work out. Just modify them as needed, in line with your current circumstances and season of life. Remember: There is no right or wrong way to spend time with Jesus. The goal is to find what works for you and God and become intentional with that path of life.

QUESTIONS

For Meditation and Discussion

1. Do you have a prayer routine?

2. What affects how often or how little you pray?

3. What form of prayer helps you become more loving toward others?

4. Are there any changes you desire to make with regard to your prayer life?

5. How can the "Five W's" help focus your prayer time and make it more fruitful?

6. Why is prayer so vital to the following:
    - Overcoming vice and growing in virtue
    - Deepening our relationship with Jesus and the Church
    - Joyfully serving others according to our state of life
    - Helping others experience God's love through us

EPILOGUE

As I end these reflections, I would like to emphasize that intentionally placing ourselves in postures that are conducive to receiving the love of Jesus is not easy. God knew us before we were formed. He created us to live in cultures that are constantly changing and that often oppose his will—yet he calls every human being to holiness. Jesus tells us to follow him. This is a narrow path, a path of obedience.

There will be seasons in our walk toward eternity where we are more faithful to following Jesus than others. I certainly have not "made it" yet, wherever "it" is. I still struggle to consistently open my heart to the love of Christ. However, I can say with all sincerity that it is when I have been consistent and intentional in my time with Jesus—even in the midst of my ongoing struggle with vice and virtue—that I have been able to radically love others, despite their imperfections. When I pray with regularity, I truly desire to remain in relationship not only with the saints in heaven but also with my fellow sinners in the body of Christ, the Church.

The Church cannot separate herself from us. Her fundamental vocation is to be "the universal sacrament of salvation"[1] In all of the stories I shared throughout this book, there is a common denominator. When we accept God's transformative love, wherever we are in our walk with him, we become open to

---

[1]   Second Vatican Council, Dogmatic Constitution on the Church, *Lumen Gentium*, 48.

sharing that Christ-like love with the members of the Church Jesus founded two thousand years ago. Like you and me, every Catholic struggles with hospitality, reconciliation, and unity. Like you and me, every Catholic struggles to keep Christ as the center of his or her life.

If you have left the Church or are struggling with your place in the body of Christ, I invite you to join me in "leaning in" to Jesus in the Eucharist and the Sacred Scriptures so that he can give us the grace to imitate him—and give us the grace to dwell with the members of the body of Christ in good times and bad.

I need you. The Church needs you. Jesus needs you.

In the midst of my own brokenness, I consider myself blessed to be able to walk with you with Jesus in this life and hopefully for all eternity in heaven.

APPENDIX
Praying the Rosary

As you hold a set of rosary beads, you will notice a crucifix, then a single bead, followed by three beads; then, there is a circle of beads in five sets (called "decades")—each with a single bead, followed by ten beads. Praying an entire Rosary, then, means praying five "decades," or one set of "mysteries."

The four sets of mysteries of the Rosary are:

The Joyful Mysteries *(prayed on Mondays and Saturdays)*

1. **The Annunciation** (Luke 1:26-38)

2. **The Visitation** (Luke 1:39-56)

3. **The Birth of Jesus** (Luke 2:1-21)

4. **The Presentation of Our Lord in the Temple** (Luke 2:22- 38)

5. **The Finding of the Child Jesus in the Temple** (Luke 2:41- 52)

The Sorrowful Mysteries *(prayed on Tuesdays and Fridays)*

1. The Agony of Our Lord in the Garden
   (Matthew 26:36-56)

2. The Scourging at the Pillar (Matthew 27:26)

3. The Crowning with Thorns (Matthew 27:27-31)

4. The Carrying of the Cross (Matthew 27:32)

5. The Crucifixion (Matthew 27:33-56)

The Glorious Mysteries *(prayed on Wednesdays and Sundays)*

1. The Resurrection (John 20:1-29)

2. The Ascension (Luke 24:36-53)

3. The Descent of the Holy Spirit (Acts 2:1-41)

4. The Assumption of Mary (see *Munificentissimus Deus,*
   Pope Pius XII, 1950)

5. The Crowning of Mary as Queen of Heaven and Earth
   (Revelation 12:1)

The Luminous Mysteries *(prayed on Thursdays)*

1. The Baptism of Our Lord (Matthew 3:13-17)

2. The Wedding Feast at Cana (John 2:1-11)

3. The Proclamation of the Kingdom of Heaven
   (Mark 1:14-15)

4. The Transfiguration (Matthew 17:1-8)

5. The Institution of the Holy Eucharist (Matthew 26)

Begin by making the Sign of the Cross, saying, "In the name of the Father, and of the Son, and of the Holy Spirit. Amen."

Then, with your fingers on the crucifix, proclaim the Apostles' Creed, a proclamation of what we believe as Christians, written in the early Church.

The Apostles' Creed

I believe in God, the Father almighty, Creator of heaven and earth, and in Jesus Christ, his only Son, our Lord, who was conceived by the Holy Spirit, born of the Virgin Mary, suffered under Pontius Pilate, was crucified, died and was buried; he descended into hell; on the third day he rose again from the dead; he ascended into heaven, and is seated at the right hand of God the Father almighty; from there he will come to judge the living and the dead. I believe in the Holy Spirit, the holy catholic Church, the communion of saints, the forgiveness of sins, the resurrection of the body, and life everlasting. Amen.

On the first single bead, pray the Our Father.

Our Father

Our Father, who art in heaven, hallowed be thy name; thy kingdom come, thy will be done, on earth as it is in heaven. Give us this day our daily bread, and forgive us our trespasses as we forgive those who trespass against us; and lead us not into temptation, but deliver us from evil. Amen.

On each of the next three beads, we pray a Hail Mary, asking for an increase in the virtues of faith, hope, and love we received in baptism.

Hail Mary

Hail Mary, full of grace, the Lord is with thee. Blessed art thou among women, and blessed is the fruit of thy womb, Jesus. Holy Mary, Mother of God, pray for us sinners, now and at the hour of our death. Amen.

On the next bead, we pray a Glory Be to honor the Holy Trinity.

Glory Be

Glory be to the Father, and to the Son, and to the Holy Spirit, as it was in the beginning, is now, and ever shall be, world without end. Amen.

Following the Glory Be, it has become traditional to pray the prayer Mary gave us at Fatima, O My Jesus.

O, My Jesus

O my Jesus, forgive us our sins, save us from the fires of hell, and lead all souls to heaven, especially those in most need of thy mercy. Amen.

Now, moving on to the five sets of "circle" beads, we meditate on a particular set of mysteries. These are key events in the life of Christ. As we saw above, there are four sets of mysteries, each of which is traditionally prayed on a different day.

On the single bead, announce the first mystery, then pray an Our Father, followed by ten Hail Marys (on each of the ten beads); then conclude with a Glory Be and an O My Jesus. Then move on to the next mystery, praying an Our Father on the next single bead, followed by ten Hail Marys, etc.

In order to enter more fully into the life of Jesus, it can be helpful to add statements of faith from the Scriptures. The following example of this practice uses the Gospel account of the Transfiguration:

And after six days Jesus took with him Peter and James and John his brother, and led them up a high mountain apart. And he was transfigured before them, and his face shone like the sun, and his garments became white as light. And behold, there appeared to them Moses and Elijah, talking with him. And Peter said to Jesus, "Lord, it is well that we are here; if you wish, I will make three booths here, one for you and one for Moses and one for Elijah." He was still speaking, when lo, a bright cloud overshadowed them, and a voice from the cloud said, "This is my beloved Son, with whom I am well pleased; listen to him." When the disciples heard this, they fell on their faces, and were filled with awe. But Jesus came and touched them, saying, "Rise, and have no fear." And when they lifted up their eyes, they saw no one but Jesus only (Matthew 17:1-8).

After we recite all five mysteries, we conclude the Rosary by praying the Hail, Holy Queen prayer. This is our final request to Mary to help us follow Jesus so that we can walk more closely with Jesus and be made worthy to enter eternal life.

Hail, Holy Queen

Hail, Holy Queen, Mother of mercy, our life, our sweetness, and our hope. To thee do we cry, poor banished children of Eve; to thee do we send up our sighs, mourning and weeping in this valley of tears. Turn then, most gracious advocate, thine eyes of mercy toward us, and after this, our exile, show unto us the blessed fruit of thy womb, Jesus. O clement, O loving, O sweet Virgin Mary! Pray for us, O Holy Mother of God. That we may be made worthy of the promises of Christ.

Also from **Ascension**

Catholic Bible

A Completely **Unique Bible** that Brings Salvation History to Life

With commentary from the creator of The Great Adventure,
Jeff Cavins, and renowned Scripture scholars
Mary Healy, Andrew Swafford, and Peter Williamson

Every Catholic needs this Bible! *The Great Adventure Catholic Bible* makes the complexity of reading the Bible simple. The narrative approach gives the big picture of salvation history and shows how everything ties together. This is the only Bible that incorporates *The Great Adventure's* color-coded *Bible Timeline*™ Learning System, a system that has made *The Great Adventure* the most popular and influential Bible study program in the English-speaking world. The color-coded tools make it easy to read and easy to remember. Truly a "game changer"! There has never been another Bible like it.

ascensionpress.com

Also from **Ascension**

A **Completely Online Series**
that Will Build Communities and Strengthen Your Faith

Featuring Michael Gormley,
co-host of **Catching Foxes** *podcast*

Following Jesus can be difficult, especially in today's world, and it is especially difficult in isolation. For many years, author and speaker Michael Gormley has been helping people come together, form groups, and grow in friendship with each other and Christ. **Don't Walk Alone** is the first in a series of programs designed specifically to build Christ-centered friendships and groups. Get two or three people together, download the free videos and discussion questions, and start having meaningful conversations—together.

ascensionpress.com

Also from **Ascension**

Understand What We Say and Do in the **Liturgy**

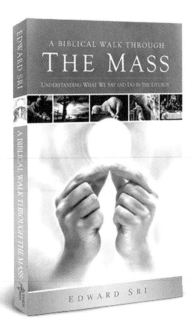

A Biblical Walk Through the Mass *by Dr. Edward Sri*

As Catholics, the Mass is the center of our Faith. We celebrate it every day. We know all the responses. We know all the gestures. But do we know what it all means?

In *A Biblical Walk Through the Mass*, Dr. Edward Sri takes us on a unique tour of the Liturgy. This book explores the biblical roots of the words and gestures we experience in the Mass and explains their profound significance. This intriguing book will renew your faith and deepen your devotion to the Eucharist.

ascensionpress.com